JACKIE BOUVIER KENNEDY

Biography

Through the Lens of Youth

D1733492

Darlene Leticia Garcia

CONTENTS

PART 1

"Read, then think. Listen, then think. Watch, then think. Think—then speak."

—*JACKIE'S ADVICE TO HER FRIEND VIVI CRESPI*

CHAPTER 1

TERRIFIC CAMERA

As the June 1949 wedding season neared, it appeared that every one of her fellow Social Register debutantes was looking for a partner. Jacqueline Bouvier only desired a "terrific camera." The final exam period at Vassar College had only just begun, but the sophomore in slender skirts, who had her long, chestnut hair straightened to drape over one of her dazzling hazel eyes, was eager to finish her second year and put the Hudson River Valley school behind. Jackie was a great student who despised school, one of her many and obvious paradoxes.

She had hurried down to the annual formal Mrs. Shippen's Dancing Class ball in Washington and the Virginia Gold Cup horse race in Warrenton, Virginia, in the weeks before she ended the Vassar semester, but "swamped with work," she then disciplined herself to study "till exams are over." She was named to the honour roll yet again. On the last day of her sophomore year, June 9, she left campus with everything she possessed.

Her destination was Merrywood, her mother and stepfather's estate in McLean, Virginia. On the way, she would almost always stop at "that camera store by the station," almost certainly Peerless Camera, which was located at 138 East 44th Street, a short walk from Grand Central, and famously offered photographers the full spectrum of new cameras and cutting-edge equipment of seemingly all makes and models, as well as an array of attachments ranging from lenses to flashes. The Leica IIc (notable for its rapid shutter speeds) that had gone into production the previous year was the object of her ambition. She had to ask the irritated clerks the same question she had asked the previous time she had stopped in: had the price of the Leica IIc come down yet? No, it had not and would not, was the consistent response. She persisted in asking, as if by sheer willpower she might cut the price of that camera. She desired the best camera to document her next year abroad in Paris.

Jackie was only a teenager when she prepared to travel to Paris that summer of 1949, but she had long been thinking like an adult; she had a desire to chart her own path and rise and fall based on her decisions. It wasn't that she couldn't enjoy her friends' activities or conform when she recognized the benefit in doing so. She wasn't trying to be a sceptic. She simply made the most of life by forging her own path. Jackie eagerly attended wedding after wedding during the summer, relieved not to be a bride herself. She had openly stated her unorthodox decision to resist the altar at the age of eighteen, understanding what postwar marriage meant for women. In her 1947 high school graduation yearbook, under "Ambition," she wrote five stark words: "Not to be a housewife." She advised a friend whose boyfriend was unsure about marriage because young men "don't want to be tied down before they've had a chance to make a good start in the world in business." She also encouraged Yusha not to "consider getting married soon," claiming that "getting married while still in college hurts people terribly."

Jackie had her bags for Paris transported to Newport before she ultimately departed Merrywood to visit her father in East Hampton. She was already worried about the lengthy time she would be apart from Yusha. "I won't see you for a minute for the next year," she said after their brief reunion in Newport at the end of summer, right before she left for Paris. Yusha, on the other hand, stayed in love with Jackie. He wrote in his diary on March 23, 1943, that as they were listening to records in the living room, he told her, "that she had a lot of sex appeal, more than anyone because she made people love to be with her and when they saw her, they had a tingle run through their veins." "I don't love her as a brother or a lover, but as a good friend who can understand and comfort me," he said three years later. I have the option of feeling sorry for myself. She lifts my spirits."

According to the account she told Yusha, Jackie kept her mother's gift of money for the camera she desired from her father. With his customary theatrics for making a statement, he didn't offer her money toward the purchase of the one she liked, but instead sent a clerk from his office to the camera shop to buy it outright for her. Jacqueline Bouvier received her Leica. After years of having her parents use her to attack one another, Jackie had become an expert at exploiting their hostility, often with a casual insinuation to one that the other had been more indulgent. Jackie didn't have to worry about them comparing notes on their gifts to her because they seldom communicated.

PART 2

EUROPE

"The only thing that breaks the monotony is breaking rules."

—JACKIE TO HER STEPBROTHER YUSHA

CHAPTER 2

PARIS

When she initially moved in, the sun set quickly in the October afternoons, and the room was cold owing to a wartime coal scarcity. She studied while "swaddled" in a "scarf, mittens, sweater, and ear muffs," the bedspread scattered with textbooks, graph-paper notebooks, airmail paper for letters home, and a variety of delicacies from surrounding patisseries. Despite the cold, she couldn't help but jump out of bed, grab her Leica, and take photos from her window. When she couldn't capture an image with her camera, she used her pen, writing letters that told the story of her travels as the American College Girl in Paris.

Her life was initially confined to her flat and the Sorbonne, which she described as a "lovely quiet grey rainy world." "I had every intention of hurling myself into the fray and emerging triumphantly laden with culture," she explained to Yusha, "and arrived loaded down with pencils & books and two pairs of glasses!" However, because of the numerous religious and municipal holidays, her teaching schedule was erratic. She also considered her course load to be "ridiculously vague." It consisted of comparative literature from the eighteenth and nineteenth centuries in English, French, and German, as well as a history class covering the Napoleonic era to World War I, but Jackie admitted she was "terrified" because it was "so complicated." Her aesthetics professor was defined as a "psychoanalyst theorist of artistic creation," and he most likely aided her developing ability to envisage and execute a sophisticated sense of personal style.

Jackie may even wear a fur coat while "being swanky at the Ritz bar" or dine with the young aristocratic French society set at the exclusive Restaurant Ledoyen. "All the boys I meet through Claude are very proper and call you Mademoiselle and have squeaking shoes and seem much too stuffy," Jackie wrote to Yusha. If you come from a nice family, they are extremely sensitive to how you act... and I go out with them quite a lot, and they show me all their little hidden nightclubs and places in Paris you'd never see if you didn't go with a Frenchman."

During some of these late-night excursions, she was exposed to a new type of music, a style of jazz that the French had created their own. The year she arrived, Paris hosted Europe's first jazz festival, and the club scene was thriving. Claude remembers accompanying her to the Club St. Germain on Rue St. Benoit and the Rose Rouge on Rue de la Harpe, where she met her Newport friend George Plimpton, a writer who was at the time active in the planning stages of the literary magazine The Paris Review with a group of American acquaintances. Plimpton was "pale, in a black turtleneck in an airless hole of a nightclub on the Boulevard Raspail," where "the blue notes of saxophones through smoke-filled haze ushered in the dawns for you, and how you would walk the grey Paris streets in the first light back to a strange bed." Jacqueline Bouvier was no nun, despite portraying herself as innocent and naive in Paris.

Not every door swung open for her. Lacking the necessary level of income to purchase the haute couture that had returned to postwar Paris design businesses, she began to dress in black more frequently, which allowed her to offer a hint toward elegant while also being practical, which was necessary given her restricted wardrobe. Jacqueline Bouvier's failed effort to sneak into a fashion show was not caused by the tiny black dress she wore. It was her digital camera.

Jackie arrived in a black gown and just expected to go into the seated, invitation-only dinner, as she subsequently told her friend, journalist Gloria Emerson. Those in charge recognized the reporters assigned to cover it, but even if she had gotten in, Jackie identified herself as an amateur by wearing her Leica around her neck and tucking a huge sketch pad under her arm—photographs and drawings were strictly prohibited. Gloria claimed that being denied access "so humiliated" Jackie that she told no one at the time, fearful that word of the incident would somehow reach Mummy and suggest that she was playing too much. As her first term at the Sorbonne came to a conclusion, she told Yusha, "I'm starting to meet lots more people, and this term is going to be even better than the last." She juggled many beaux now that she had settled confidently in Paris. Among them were an aspiring writer, an assistant to Prime Minister Georges Bidault, the son of a diplomat, and Paul de Ganay, a member of a prominent aristocratic family. One of Plimpton's "brilliant and romantic" acquaintances and the son of a Pulitzer Prize-winning author, American writer John Marquand, was a notable Paris beau. Gore Vidal would later say that Jackie "lost her virginity" to Marquand "in a lift that he had stalled in a pension on Paris's Left Bank," despite Marquand's denial. Vidal's subsequent claim that they were discussing marriage, on the other hand, contradicts everything Jackie had said about love at that period in her life "when everything was beginning." Jackie Bouvier's goal was not to be a writer's girlfriend; rather, she shared the male writers' desires "that our lives would not be mundane."

"Mostly the boys I knew were beetle-browed intellectual types who'd discuss very serious things with me," she explained. "Nothing romantic at all." She was particularly irritated by one of them back home, an American who rambled on about the French Nazi collaborator Marshal Pétain without taking into account that she'd followed the news story about his commutation and had an informed opinion. "I tried to appear intelligent and nod at the appropriate times," she recalled. "I'm no expert on anything, but he sounded like a little boy who had just finished a big book and was... expounding on it all... without really understanding what it was all about." I wanted to give him a big mother kiss... and tell him he'd grown up!"

She and Yusha had discussed dating and love in the months leading up to her trip to Paris. "As far as I can tell, you're still in the state of mind where you just can't find the right boy yet and you're getting desperate and enjoying them all, but just take it easy," he said, worried by her concurrent beau. Jackie justified her pattern of dating: "Just because I write to a boy and go on dates with him doesn't imply I love him... I don't expect to be passionately in love right now, and it's fine to like a number of people—so don't believe any boy I mention in a letter to you is my great love."

"I did love going to all the dances," Jackie said of Newport's social scene, where the frothy music of the Lester Lanin Band and the Meyer Davis Band set the tone for her 1940s summers there, as she did the rhumba or led a conga line. There were also traces of her boredom with the young men who were interested in her. "I had a feeling she was looking over my shoulder to see who her next dance partner would be," recalled one of the parquet's many possible beaus.

"When I was about nineteen, I knew I didn't want the rest of my life to be there," she said. I didn't want to marry any of the young men I grew up with, not because they were bad men, but because of their circumstances."

She got her basic white dress off the rack at a department store for her debutante tea. She became a regular at Social Register dances, dinners, luncheons, and teas after being named "Deb of the Year" four months later. She exemplified noblesse oblige by participating in the Free Milk for Babies Fund charity effort, selling tickets to benefit performances of Lucia di Lammermoor and a Verdi Festival at the Metropolitan Opera, raising funds for the Madison Square Boys' Club, and posing for a November 1947 New York Times publicity photo. She found it suffocating on the inside. "I really wanted to do the Virginia reel in the middle of the Plaza ballroom," she joked after a winter dance. Nonetheless, Jacqueline Bouvier had a public reputation that designated her as a part of the elite, thanks to her Deb of the Year status and education at Miss Porter's, Vassar, and the Sorbonne. Unk was responsible for the final touch of calling two estates home. In another letter to Yusha, she warned him not to fall in love with any one girl more than once or twice in his life, revealing her own view of commitment: "You shouldn't fall in love more than once or twice in your whole life—and don't ever try to make yourself, because then it won't ever be real." It will happen someday—and it will be lovely for both of you. What you should actually do is write to numerous girls and take out several and rush several at dances or "play the field" in the summer to see what they're all like and try not to get too involved with any of them— because you always make it seem like love in your own mind when it really isn't. And after each of those amazing romances, you're left feeling devastated and uncertain...

"If you're going to fall in love, you'll just fall—maybe in a minute standing next to her at the Snack Bar, or perhaps after a long time you'll suddenly realise you love her... Please don't try to force yourself to fall in love... It's completely incorrect." And what was correct? If her time away was giving her a feel of the type of partner she knew she didn't want, it was also giving her a sense of her perfect marriage. "I want to marry a man with imagination," she explained to her sister. "And that's not easy to find."

CHAPTER 3

THE "TERRIFIC" VACATION

The Palais Epstein was her destination. Built in 1871 as a residence for the merchant after whom it was named, and famed for its ornate interior architecture, it had served as the Soviet Kommandantura's headquarters since 1945. Massive red-starred banners representing Vladimir Lenin and Soviet leader Joseph Stalin obscured its ornate facade. By 1949, it had become "a place dreaded by many Viennese," as the Austrian government now characterises it, "the starting point of many deportees' suffering on their way to Siberia."

Soviet police were on every corner, armed with Thompson submachine guns, a weapon popularised by gangster films and FBI sleuths. They weren't frightening enough to keep Jackie from raising her Leica and photographing the edifice. She didn't seem to receive many photos. "[T]he Russians with Tommy guns in Vienna—they stopped me for taking a picture of their building and tried to get me to come in their hotel for questioning, but I wouldn't because I was afraid I'd never get out," she explained to Yusha. In fact, she didn't tell him the whole tale because she didn't want Mummy to find out the truth. (If she trusted anyone, it was Yusha, but Janet's interrogations were notoriously harsh.) She did not reveal the truth in writing until 1967, to her friend Robert McNamara, Kennedy's secretary of defence, with whom she maintained a discussion about the reality of the Cold War. Jackie remembered the experience as "the only time I have ever been scared—because they kept us inside for three hours."

After a few days in Vienna, Jackie and Martha Rusk travelled to Salzburg and Berchtesgaden, both in southeastern Germany, which Jackie claimed as "where Hitler lived," with the sole existing structure from his time there being the Mooslahnerkopf teehaus, which he visited on a daily basis. (Jackie was one of the few tourists who saw it before it was destroyed, ensuring that no building affiliated with Hitler survived.)

Rather than learning history in school, where the emphasis was on memorising facts, she had acquired an interest in the topic through art and literature, devouring innumerable biographies of British, Irish, and French monarchs, as well as their formidable spouses and paramours. She also acknowledged the importance of preserving and witnessing the areas where history had transpired. She and Martha took a ten-mile trolley ride from Munich, her final destination before Rome, to Dachau, the mediaeval town that housed the first Nazi concentration camp, where it was estimated that 41,500 people were killed. The swastika and imperial eagle that decorated the camp's main gate had been removed, but the mass murder and cremation facilities remained. Some 15,000 inmates were buried there with no markers, only warning signals of infestation and infection to those who came too close to the burial site. The new German administration had agreed to keep it as a memorial a few weeks before. When Jackie returned to Paris, she did not address Dachau with Claude, but she defended her visit to Vivi in Rome. "She had wanted to see it," Vivi explained. She was curious. She was so shocked... my Italian husband asked, 'Why would you want to see something like this?' History. She was curious about these topics."

While celebrating New Year's Eve with Jackie and several friends in a Munich nightclub, Martha Rusk saw a stark contrast between the city's shells of bombed-out buildings and the lively beer halls, as if nothing had happened there in the previous few years. While his stepsister was "appalled and outraged" by the Holocaust, Yusha maintained that she "always saw the Nazis as distinct from the German people." He pointed out that she was so taken with Germany's first chancellor, Otto von Bismarck (who oversaw the country's unification in 1871), that she later travelled to northern Germany to "touch his grave." That may have been her latter wish, but in an early 1950 letter to Yusha, she said unequivocally that "the Germans are still Nazis and have secret meetings and just think the Americans are a bunch of suckers sending them dollars."

Her travel east, with her three-hour detention in Vienna, had provided a glimpse into how catastrophic life could be under a tyrannical dictatorship. She attempted to keep her cool while being grilled by the Soviets, who were trying to figure out if she was on an espionage mission, while she was kept sat, staring at a blank wall except for a giant, intimidating portrait of Stalin.

When she told Yusha about it months later, she described her experiences at Dachau and Vienna "the most terrific vacation," adding that she'd "really gotten in there and saw what it is like." What she feared about being taken to Siberia was nothing compared to the immediate peril she would face in a month.

"Stalin doesn't scare me half as much as Mummy," Jackie joked.

CHAPTER 4

LIBERTÉ

Jackie's frenetic, convoluted account to Yusha in the Louvre was so accurate that he remembered every detail. Jackie walked him all the way up to the Grande Galerie, to the ninth panel, where Titian's Woman with a Mirror and Allegory of Marriage are shown. With her typical, enigmatic smile, she was restricted behind a bench and a low rope against a wall. Jackie Bouvier had stood months previously, on a dimly lit winter afternoon, peering at the Mona Lisa, poised to raise her Leica. So her story for Yusha started. Jackie pursued the Mona Lisa with her camera, encroaching on its bounds and jeopardising its protection. An elderly guard, one of 214 "retired soldiers or disabled war veterans" in charge of the entire museum, hobbled over as swiftly as he could to save the embattled, adored symbol from the camera-wielding girl. She took a step back, loudly apologising. Her primary goal had been to disprove the widely held assumption that the Mona Lisa's gaze was always fixated on the person staring at her.

The guard wheeled angrily and waddled back to his post at the far end of the gallery, mumbling "Américaines arrogantes" loud enough for her to hear. "Who do you think you think you are?"

Jackie justified her actions by arguing that she needed to keep photographing from different perspectives because she wouldn't know if she had succeeded until the film was developed, so she brought her Leica closer to the canvas, ignored the rope, and nearly climbed up on the bench. "She knew she was being naughty," Yusha observed, but it seemed justified: "He was being mean to say that." "What exactly does being an American have to do with it?"

Jackie took a deep breath and waited at the top of a curved marble staircase before slowly descending the steps while rising tourists looked on and divided to the sides. "Anyone can make an entrance," she continued, standing next to Yusha on the same stairwell, "but the real art is making an exit."

According to Yusha, they went "up the Eiffel Tower, up and down the Champs-Élysées, along the banks of the Seine, through the Bois de Boulogne, and the Tuileries Garden, Notre-Dame, Maxim's, having pressed duck at the Tour D'Argent, and Versailles." She pointed to the location in the Versailles Hall of Mirrors where she made her public debut in French. "What don't you see here?" she asked, looking around. He gazed at the furniture and historical figure busts. She said, "There's not one woman—but they were important too."

She walked around Paris with her Leica, exhibiting how light changed the shape of Louvre sculptures, accentuated the hues of yellow in the Tuileries' dahlia beds, and exposed the hidden patterns of the Eiffel Tower's interconnected timbers. She wasn't sure which format she favoured. Although black and white photography can depict journalistic reality, as she said to George Plimpton, "the greys and silvers disguise as much as they tell."

Jackie Bouvier's name and face had been in the media since she was a child, so she was used to constructing a public persona, learning how to be "on," to make a purposeful impression, to manufacture herself into a character. Her commentary was now a part of the scene. Her stories took on an episodic quality as a result of her narrating, chronicling, romanticising, mythologizing, and, most importantly, editing, in which she presented herself as the hapless protagonist in some zany predicament, blending what confidante Nancy "Tucky" Tuckerman called a "sense of the ridiculous" with enough detail to set the stage and capture the essence of the characters she met. It's tough to say how much of her stories were based on her genuine self-perception vs the image she wanted others to see. Yusha didn't care how much of her Mona Lisa or other strange legends she had embroidered. It was another evidence of her "capacity for concentration," which he found best "exhibited in amusing storytelling, both real and imaginative."

Yusha drove off to the south of France with Claude's friend Solange Batsell, a French attorney who had studied in the United States, at the start of their summer vacation. Yusha, the romantic, had fallen head over heels for her, and the two intended to spend some time alone together. Jackie travelled to Lyon to meet Claude, who was driving her sister's automobile. Beginning on July 15, Jackie and Claude set off on a road journey through the most distant and ancient communities of south-central and coastal "deep France." For her, it was a rustic experience because they would "picnic in the woods, swim in a river, and go fishing." The facilities were basic. She, like everyone else, used the outhouses. They began their journey with a leisurely study of the Auvergne region's undulating hills, "the part of France where relatively few visitors travel... covered with fields and old people with cows and hammers where the butcher and baker pass with a truck once a week... "There's a ruined chateau on every hill," she wrote Mummy. They came across big public washing ponds on the outskirts of the mediaeval village of Salers, with clotheslines carrying goods drying in the sun. Jackie took some laundry and "decided to finish the job as a good washer-woman," soaking the clothing and scrubbing each item while kneeling on the stone perimeter.

They visited the church in the half-deserted village of Conques, where visitors previously left relics and jewellery. They fished for trout in the tiny river and rode narrow canal boats driven by horses down the accompanying road through the Gorges du Tarn, where centuries-old hamlets still clung to the steep slopes. As the sun fell that day, Jackie got into her bathing suit and imitated Esther Williams. They swam and sunbathed in a real pool and a deeper river in Toulouse. "We both realised thatV it was a time of freedom," Claude said, "getting some sense of ourselves."

Their only plan was to meet Yusha and Solange in Saint-Jean-de-Luz, a short drive from the Spanish border, at the end of July. Their friend Donald Coons had rented "Borda-Berri," an opulent manor house, for the summer, and they were joined by other friends, Gordon Wholey, Freaky Vreeland (son of famous fashion editor Diana Vreeland), and Demi Gates, the brother of her friend Puffin. Jackie celebrated her 21st birthday with them, marking her passage into adulthood. To allay any fears about the rite of passage, she celebrated it informally by wearing shorts, playing tennis, and winning a bike race.

Jackie, Claude, Yusha, and Solange drove north toward Bordeaux, stopping at the Château de La Brède, "where Montesquieu wrote his political works on democracy," Claude recalled, and there was "[a]moment of emotion in his library" as they perused documents tangentially related to the establishment of the United States. They visited Saintes and its famed Gothic basilica before continuing on to La Rochelle. They stopped in Nantes after viewing the island of Marmoutier off the coast of Brittany, where they spoke with a nun about "her dedication to lonesome children," Claude recounted. The following stop, La Bretesche, was particularly remarkable. "We arrived late in the afternoon and wandered until late at night around the moat and grounds," Claude wrote. After crossing a historic drawbridge into a castle, they imagined they saw "the ghosts of the arrowed knights fighting each other behind the cedar trees." Then they went to Azay-le-Rideau to view the famed fifteenth-century island château that appeared to rise straight out of the ocean. There was one last picnic along the Loire, complete with sandwiches, grapes, and wine. They eventually returned to Paris. Jackie still had several weeks of travel ahead of her, but Mummy made a public proclamation of her impending return, maybe to dissuade her from inventing any excuse to delay her return longer. She had her acquaintance, society journalist Betty Beale (no relation to Black Jack's sister's family), declare in the July 5, 1950, Washington Evening Star that "Jacqueline Bouvier, post deb... is returning to the Capital [winter social] scene next year... Jackie enjoys Paris and is sad to leave there, but she is returning to complete her final year at George Washington."

Yusha and Jackie arrived in Dublin on Monday, August 14, 1950, just in time for the city's annual horse show's final day. They tried to contact a close literary friend of Uncle Lefty's, Father Joseph Leonard, for assistance, but he was out of town. Jackie immediately went to the American Embassy and appealed for help. Aides not only secured them accommodations, but also lent them a car for their time in Ireland. The next day, Father Leonard returned to Dublin and escorted them to every sight they desired to visit. He instantly linked with Jackie over their similar love of books, the age difference immaterial to his admiration for her brain.

Leonard piqued her interest in the lives of Ireland's most celebrated and politically subversive writers by visiting locations linked with James Joyce, William Butler Yeats, Samuel Beckett, Bram Stoker, and Oscar Wilde. He took them to see George Bernard Shaw's play The Doctor's Dilemma at the Abbey Theatre one evening. There was lunch at Restaurant Jammet, which was described in Joyce's Ulysses, and a Guinness-fueled pub night.

Leonard even arranged for them to meet with his friend, Irish Prime Minister John A. Costello, who remembered Jackie as "full of youthful vivacity and charm" and "delighted with everything she found in Ireland." She also met Costello's son Declan, a young attorney three years her senior, at the American Embassy. Jackie fell head over heels for the future Attorney General of Ireland, telling Father Leonard that he was "absolutely heaven." There wasn't time for anything meaningful to grow, but they'd be friends for life.

They spent a lot of time outside, visiting the city's architecture as well as Phoenix Park, which has wild deer as well as cricket, polo, and hurling fields. Jackie had two regrets about her stay in Dublin: not being able to "shake hands with the mummy" preserved in the thousand-year-old St. Michan's Church and, as she informed Yusha the day before they left, not being there during Easter, which "would have been so meaningful." Her meaning became evident when she began counting the number of Irish individuals jailed, wounded, dead, and executed during the "Easter Uprising" for independence from the "bloodthirsty" English, as well as reciting lines from Yeats's "Easter 1916." "The more she travelled in Ireland," Yusha observed, "the more she wanted to be Irish."

Jackie's conduct varied while Yusha drove (Dublin to Kildare, Kilkenny, Waterford, Cobh, Cork, Blarney, Killarney, Limerick, and Tipperary). Yusha recalls her falling into silent reading at times, "always studying the complicated [Irish] history," "crazy about the Irish kings." At times, when she passed by the remnants of fortified castles, she delivered a running monologue about Irish history, integrating her "knowledge of art and architecture as well as military history." She was particularly captivated by the environment in various shades of green.

Every day of their "three joyful weeks," as they strolled down one-lane roads to one tiny village after another, Jackie played fully assigned historical and literary character attributes to the real individuals they met. A strong milkmaid was transformed into "Molly Pitcher," a patronising mechanic into "Julius Caesar," and a proud, pallid young farmhand into "Wilfred of Ivanhoe." Yusha found her odd, obscure comments hysterical, but also revelatory of her capacity to recognize timeless human connections, which has become an increasingly recognizable feature of her humour. Her year in Europe exposed her to so many diverse cultures that she inevitably lost a lot of the prejudice she had carried with her. "Her stay in France had been a broadening experience," Yusha told a reporter a decade later. "She had met so many people

PART 3

WRITING

"I could be a sort of Overall Art Director of the Twentieth Century, watching everything from a chair hanging in space."

—JACKIE, IN AN ESSAY FOR VOGUE

CHAPTER 5

GEORGE WASHINGTON UNIVERSITY

Jacqueline Bouvier began her first day at George Washington University on October 2, 1950, travelling around the urban campus in D.C.'s Foggy Bottom district. She was transferring majors, which meant she would have a harder burden. Her class was 40% female, but her determination to graduate made her an exception in an era when those who obtained a diploma rather than a fiancée were deemed socially failed. Despite the fact that she had to live under Mummy's thumb and commute to school, GWU proved to be an ideal place for her. Jackie began her time at GWU on purpose, in the office of an assistant dean, seeking permission to change her major from English to French literature with a minor in art, and consulting on what classes she required to do so. She began her studies immediately after that. She accompanied her presentations in art history class with colour slides she photographed at the Louvre and subsequently contributed to the art department. Jackie obtained permission to go above and beyond expectations in her French literature class, where students were supposed to research and compose reports in English on works by France's best writers.

On the day of the deadline, OCTOBER 10, Jackie completed her application for the Vogue contest and submitted it in, along with a note to the contest director, Mary Campbell. She lied about the application's late delivery, saying, "I returned from Europe only a week ago and then it took me several days to get hold of an August issue of Vogue as there were none left on the newsstands." In reality, she had returned on September 12, and Mummy had given her that Vogue issue two weeks later. She told a second lie, saying she "completed three years at Vassar" but without mentioning the Sorbonne, possibly because she thought editors would prefer applicants who had never lived in Paris.

Fearing that Vogue would reject her application owing to its lateness, she attempted to demonstrate her worth by declaring she would "go ahead" and compose the first round of essays—due November 1— even before they determined whether the application would be accepted. Her application was accepted, which she was relieved about, but two and a half weeks later, on October 31, she emailed Campbell again, "ashamed to be asking for an extension" for her first round of essays. While she acknowledged that "it was stupid of me not to have gotten them done way ahead of the deadline," she blamed the delay on a student she paid to type the four essays. She apparently forgot her prior claim that she'd begun writing weeks earlier when she claimed to have handwritten the thirteen thousand words of flowing prose in just four days. Whether Campbell realised it or not, she accepted Jackie's articles when they arrived on November 3. Despite her shaky start, Jackie's willingness to risk disqualification by committing a few lies demonstrated how badly she wanted to write—and return to Paris. Jackie chose poets Charles Baudelaire, Oscar Wilde, and ballet director Serge Diaghilev for her essay on people she wished she had met. She revealed a great understanding of the creative process in it. According to her study, "a common theory runs through their work, a certain concept of the intersection of the arts," and she provocatively stated that these artists shared "a belief that beauty in art has nothing to do with questions of good or evil."

Baudelaire and Wilde were "idealists who could paint their sinfulness with honesty," and Wilde had the ability to capture the late Victorian era "with the flash of an epigram." She identified Baudelaire's "theory of synesthesia, a tendency to associate the impressions given by one of the senses with those given by another." Jackie did it, as evidenced by her vivid descriptions of Wilde's "sensory images" in her essay: "...the yellow liquid light pools in the street cut by the stiletto tree branches outside the Harlot's House, the musk of gold heat that emanates from a vase of flowers in the Music Room."

Diaghilev was featured because of the way he mixed Eastern and Western cultural components in his ballets. She would also famously imitate a unique quality he possessed: "[H]e possessed what is rarer than artistic genius in any one field; the sensitivity to take the best of each man and incorporate it into a masterpiece all the more precious because it lives only in the minds of those who have seen it and disintegrates as soon as he is gone."

Jackie ended with a fantasy assertion of her ideal function in the greater world: "Overall Art Director of the Twentieth Century, watching everything from a chair hanging in space."

Her biographical profile was more intimate, needing impartiality regarding her strengths and weaknesses. After conceding, "I do not have a sensational figure but can look slim if I pick the right clothes," she named her literary idols as Mowgli from The Jungle Book, Scarlett O'Hara from Gone with the Wind, Earl of Dorincourt from Little Lord Fauntleroy, and Robin Hood. Her other secret location was Unk's library, where she read through his old books on literature, history, philosophy, and architecture. Jackie was initially drawn to a shelf of many leather-bound volumes by Alexandre Dumas, which she read in order. "I can remember a slight commotion when I lost volume twenty-one," she recounted, "but I found it somewhere."

She made friendships with the house staff, who were often her only companions in the home; during her first journey to Europe, she brought each a present, from rosary beads blessed by the Pope for the Irish cook to gloves for an elderly butler. She enjoyed visiting the stables with Doc, the family's handyman and horse groomer, since he was "wonderful at spitting tobacco." She dubbed a Scottie puppy she presented to Mummy in a hatbox "Corkscrew," a cheeky reference to Doc, who she knew sipped whiskey from a flask. Over time, the family had about six pets. Aside from Corkscrew, there were poodles Caprice and Gally, a Great Dane Ellita, and a Welsh terrier Woofty at Merrywood, and she studied their different personalities; having them in her room while she worked calmed her down. Merrywood was most at ease in the wider natural world.

CHAPTER 6

LAST SEMESTER

With temperatures in Washington averaging 48 degrees in the first two months of 1951, Jackie would dash outside in slacks and a turtleneck sweater and mount the fearsome Chief or the erratic Sagebrush to gallop hard or meander slowly across Merrywood, from the shooting range to the forest of black walnut trees that had supplied the library's wood panelling. She then gratefully brushed her beloved beasts in their stable. Jackie viewed horses to be friends, whereas Janet rated them by how skillfully they transported her from one silver award to the next. Jackie could indulge her other favourite getaway anyplace if she could only ride consistently at Merrywood. Jackie likes reading two novels at once, preferably from different genres. She read Hemingway, Twain, Poe, Hawthorne, and Maugham, as well as obscure new authors. George Plimpton recalls her recommending Jack Kerouac's The Town and the City long before he became famous. She enjoyed rereading "my treasures," she told Yusha the previous fall, asking him to retrieve her "tiny little art and ballet books—Shakespeare, etc." from Newport storage. She was conversant with most of French literature. When journalist Richard Lemon informed her about an obscure new translation of François-René de Chateaubriand's writings, she not only knew about it but also told him that "his novels were romantic and fluffy."

Her strong attention to the Vogue writings, on the other hand, irritated both of her parents. Black Jack waited for the phone call she always made to him on New Year's Day, but it never arrived. His nephew recalled that his uncle's "thoughtlessness was crushing," leaving him "feeling abandoned and alone." Mummy also claimed that Jackie was wasting her time because no affluent man would marry an intellectual lady. Janet not only "criticised her love of books and learning," as one of Jackie's chroniclers later put it, but she also believed that if Jackie did not begin to "conceal how bright she was," she would never "land a husband."

Mummy could have been right if Jackie had aspired to be a wife rather than a writer. Her following series of pieces, however, demanded a change. The first round gave a feel of who she was, but the second round demanded a technical and professional tone, hinting at the type of Vogue editor she might be. She produced an original short narrative about Grumpy Jack's funeral, an opinion article on how to best visually display new women's clothing, another opinion piece on men's fashion, and then a critique of Vogue's December perfume story, along with her own alternative version. In her debut opinion post, she said that Vogue should primarily employ a professional model to highlight new styles, who should "efface herself and call attention to her dress," and that photographers should catch "the cut, fabric, and detail of a dress." She proposed that the magazine give its fashion images a "moved-up-to-the-1950s" look by replicating the work of early-twentieth-century artist Kees van Dongen, whose style she acknowledged copying in her own paintings, revealing her breadth of artistic expertise. Although she admitted that it would be "fun to come across Marlene Dietrich brooding in a great black cape on occasion," she concluded that "obnoxious as the clink of silver may be, Vogue could not exist if the clothes it featured did not sell."

In her second opinion column, she offered a "new approach for Vogue on the subject of men's fashions," demonstrating the attentiveness she inherited from her fashionable father as well as her skill for method, branding, and marketing. Men's fashion would always be dominated by Esquire, thus Vogue articles on men's fashion should be "directed at women" who can assist men in creating a wardrobe that, while "bound by convention and good taste," can reflect "colour, variety, and elegance." She suggested articles about shirts, collars, cuffs, ties, suspenders, and suits, as well as a regular feature of two facing pages of images of one well-dressed and one poorly dressed renowned man. She made the feminist case that women should not be held accountable for how men dress, and that men should learn to dress for themselves.

Jackie's last piece was a rebuttal to Vogue's December cover story, "Famous Noses, Famous Scents." She praised the "eye-catching, appropriate, and original" layout of black-and-white photos of noses at the top of the page. She warned that, despite its "shock power," viewers might forget the perfume bottle illustrations at the bottom. She provided her own extensive explanation, combining her knowledge of history, literature, and the senses. She began with the idea that perfume was "analogous to wine," because both "act upon the closely related senses of taste and smell to produce an intoxicating effect," and advised combining perfume poetry with wine literature, ranging from "Omar Khayyam to Colonel Cantwell and Renata."

She planned a two-page spread for her perfume and poetry section. She wanted some brief writing relating perfume and literature in the upper-right-hand corner of the left page, as well as "a full-page photograph of a finely-grained bookshelf filled with thin bound and toled volumes," with bottles of perfume between the books. "In colour, it could be quite effective, with the red, green, and gold of the books, the sheen of the wood, and the liquid amber sealed inside beautifully cut bottles." On the right, she imagined a snapshot of an open book "with parchment pages for texture interest," next to an open perfume bottle. She wanted three quotes about poetry, across both pages: from Milton's Samson Agonistes ("Coveted by all the winds that hold them play / An amber accent of odorous perfume / Her harbinger"); Shakespeare's Hamlet ("A violet in the youth of my primy nature / Forward, not permanent sweet, not lasting / The perfume and suppliance of a minute"); and a poem of Oscar Wilde's ("And the perfume of your soul / Is vague and suffusing / with the pungence of sealed spice jars"). Jackie made a few mistakes with these quotes for her essay in her haste. In the proper Milton quotation, "Coveted" should be "Courted," and the poem she labelled as Oscar Wilde was actually an excerpt from Amy Lowell's "A Lady."

She imagined a similar layout for her take on wine and perfume, with the headline "Intoxicating Liquids" or "The Petal and the Grape." She wanted some quick opening text in the left page's right-hand corner, like she did on the first spread, with a massive background image of wine-cellar compartments with perfume bottles branded like wine bottles in each. She proposed doing it in black and white, with "the black depths of the compartments pointing up the reflections of the glass bottles." On the right, over black, she wanted "strewn flower petals," with a hazy sense of a woman pouring perfume from a "diorama bottle" into a thin-stemmed crystal wine glass. She finished her final semester of college after submitting her essays by the January 15 deadline. For a graduating senior, it was a demanding course load. She enrolled in a journalism writing class because, as she subsequently told Molly Thayer, "I wanted to get to know people better." I felt studying journalism would be a fantastic opportunity." Other courses she took included Man in Modern Society, Readings for the Major in French Literature, and Development of European Civilization, whose lecturer, Dean Elmer Louis Kayser, she described as a "most incredible teacher." After a few weeks of economics class, she "decided I wasn't up to [it]," she subsequently revealed. Finance and business bore her to tears. Muriel McClanahan, who taught Bouvier's advanced English composition course, Short Story, fondly recalled how Bouvier "always sat in the back of the classroom" next to a French-Canadian student, Joe Metivier, so they could whisper during class, "always in French." Jackie and she developed a warm mutual regard. Jackie would not have been able to afford rent on even a modest apartment and meet her living expenses with her monthly $545 allowance from Black Jack. She was also unable to live on a budget. She disguised her shame by overdrawing her account by inadvertently writing bogus checks at boarding school, despite the fact that she faced a $1,000 fine and jail time if detected. "I'm waiting for the cops to catch me," she explained to Yusha, "but I only had about 50 cents anyway." She may have complained about Mummy's "keeping me in the home," but it was a mansion with servants to cook and clean for her.

Many of her acquaintances now had wealthy husbands who supported them rather than their parents. Her future husband would need to be extremely wealthy in order for her to maintain her privileged lifestyle by marrying. If he was a contemporary, as most of her beaux had been, he would have to be either extraordinarily successful in his field or heir to a fortune, or an older, independently wealthy man. This did not even address what Jackie considered to be the most important problem of compatibility: given her uncommon level of brilliance for a woman of any class at the time, Jackie would have been content with someone of equal or more intelligence, curiosity, and desire for knowledge. Her Catholicism complicated matters in a dating pool dominated by Protestants; families of both faiths still wanted their children to marry someone of the same denomination. Furthermore, the pressure from both parents meant that her ideal prospective husband would have the status that they valued—ancestry, selective boarding school and college educations, exclusive club memberships, powerful social and business connections, and a favourable position in a respected profession with a high income.

Jacqueline Bouvier's final Vogue contribution was a miniature work of art. With "Nostalgia" as her theme, she wrote an opening editorial before outlining six fashion and five feature articles. She was "evoking the past," not re-creating it, with a cover image of a drawing by frequent Vogue illustrator Eugene Berman meant to "capture the romanticism of the far-off and bygone." She started with six different types of fashion pieces.

The largest of these featured costumes: a Scottish Sherlock Holmes cape; an Imperial Russian fox-collar tunic coat; a trumpet skirt and bolero jacket resembling a Spanish riding habit; a buttoned cape cut like a priest's cassock; a massive red taffeta dress, coat, and pillbox hat that looked like it could belong to a Venetian cardinal; a tight-fitting jacket with bows like those worn

The second exhibition, "Echo the Ages in the Evening," featured colourful gowns worn by famous women of the time, including Nehru's wife, Kamala, in a stylized sari on an Indian prayer rug, Princess Alexandra of Greece in a calla lily tunic next to a classical statue, and socialite Babe Paley in an Edwardian-style gown next to a Sargent portrait.

"Moments for Memories" was her third fashion article, and it featured a two-page spread of white "enormously full skirted" wedding and debutante dresses photographed against a black background with white type, clothes that would be preserved in "folds of tissue paper" to be "your own very special piece of nostalgia." The second one, "For the Girl with More Taste than Money," was aimed at those who couldn't afford Vogue's high-end couture. It included a "sleeveless sheath with scooped neckline" and, in a three-page black-and-white layout, showed how it might be altered using nine imaginatively varied accessories: Wearing a long-sleeved striped blouse with white collars and cuffs over it conjures up images of "the schoolgirl blouse." When paired with a "great dip brimmed black hat," it would give the impression of a "femme fatale one takes to hear tangos at teatime." By putting organza balloon shoulders to it, a woman may resemble a member of "the Corps de Ballet of Giselle." A red chiffon scarf twisted over necklaces and dozens of arm bracelets would have a woman dressed in a sheath ready to "dance the Charleston." With a short-sleeved ribbed turtleneck over the dress with wrist gloves and a beret, the wearer would "swagger like D'Artagnan." A crimson petticoat visible beneath the hem would "bring Andalucia into the living room." The sheath could be transformed into a cocktail dress with a huge "Alice in Wonderland butterfly bow" and long streamers. Draping it with a black-fringed crimson cape alluded to the Gay '90s, while wearing it with a striped taffeta apron made the wearer "feel as if you stepped out of Tales of the Arabian Nights."

Jackie offered a variety of current hats inspired by historical imagery in her fifth fashion post, including a Renaissance page's beanie, a matador's bicorne, a sailor's cap, a flapper's cloche, and a clerical calot. To evoke a nostalgic sense, her final article utilised shots of coloured garments put in larger images of colourful paintings, such as grey in a Whistler, blue in a Persian miniature, and yellow in a Gauguin.

Finally, Jackie wrote five feature articles about nostalgia. The most intriguing proposal was for an article to be written by a Proust expert who could explain his "exact science of evoking the past," using "sensory perception" (which she used herself), in which "one concentrated upon [an object] intensely" it could "set off a chain of thoughts that will put the thinker back" into a similar past situation.

The second element she proposed was the obscure F. Scott and Zelda Fitzgerald tale "Show Mr. and Mrs. F. to Number—," which she described as "beautifully written," about the sequence of hotel rooms the couple stayed in, with "echoes of the twenties." Her third feature was a collection of extracts from earlier generation humour authors such as H. L. Mencken. Her fourth submission was a "Gossipy Memo," written by an unidentified social critic and citing historical events such as the Titanic tragedy, Lindbergh's flight, Shirley Temple, and the Teapot Dome affair. Finally, she devised "Vogue Nominations for Nostalgia," which incorporated elements of modern pop culture that she believed will elicit nostalgia in twenty years, such as "television fever," the resurgence of prizefighter Joe Louis, and the Broadway musical South Pacific. Bouvier's contribution was reviewed by a dozen Vogue editors from March to April. The initial review, written on March 9 by Mrs. Gleaves, was negative: "Flat footed." The biography is uninviting. Other pieces are sensible and comprehensive. "There is no flair." The next three put her on a positive track. On March 16, Miss Talmey said, "Would definitely consider this girl—has range; easy writing; bright mind." On March 26, Miss Daves said, "Wonderful possibility." We must take her seriously." On April 5, Miss Heal said, "A. Intelligent, has a good background and a fashion sense." Following a mixed assessment ("Uneven—but some of it isn't bad"), Carol Phillips, the managing editor, gave her a "AAAAAA," declaring: "This is IT - for my vote." A very excellent collection of articles. Each paper is outstanding. There is no exception to this rule. She is a writer, and she undoubtedly has an editorial point of view. My only concern is that she might marry and ride off on one of those horses she mentions. But I'm counting on her to be a part of the copy room crew!!!"

Meanwhile, Vogue requested a background check on Jackie from GWU, which responded that she was a "very pleasing, attractive young lady," while Muriel McClanahan said she "writes much better than most students and that her critical sense is perceptive... very worthy of any honour she might win."

Jackie was ready for action while she awaited graduation and the completion of her CIA security clearance. "There hasn't been anything going on here. "It's a dreary winter day, and we're all sick," she wrote to Father Leonard. She was delighted by John Husted's undivided attention, but she still thought of him as "immature and boring."

On Tuesday, April 24, the Prix de Paris director, Mary Campbell, notified Jackie through email that "you are among the top finalists," from which the winner will be picked. Not insignificantly, Mary Campbell provided appreciation (something Jackie was unaccustomed to receiving from her own mother): "[Y]ou have done a swell job and deserve a lot of credit for the hard and painstaking work you have done." The editors, according to Campbell, thought "you had one of the most interesting papers submitted."

The finalists were invited to a dinner with Vogue editors on May 10 and a luncheon with Condé Nast executives the next day. Jackie's final comprehensive examinations clashed with the date, so she planned for a lunch date on May 3. Mary Campbell hurried her up to the Vogue offices when she arrived at the Condé Nast headquarters in the Graybar Building at 420 Lexington Avenue. Entering a workplace where words and photos were used professionally piqued her interest, especially "how alert everyone had seemed." It was the young woman's first encounter with such a situation. Jackie had first promised the Vogue editors that she would fly to New York for their lunch appointment, but she instead drove up. She hurriedly left lunch to drive ninety minutes north to Farmington to pick up her sister, who was now more focused on her upcoming first trip to Europe, with Jackie approved as chaperone by Mummy. In an audacious move to reassure the editors, she said that she was "satiated" with Paris and that what was more important to her was the work. If she succeeded, she intended to begin in January, when her commitment to the CIA project would be completed. The most eye-opening revelation in Jackie Bouvier's letter was her awakening sense of purpose, which she proceeded to pursue: "I suddenly realised what an exciting thing it must be to have something important to do."

Jackie Bouvier relaxed after finishing her final examinations, getting the CIA position that autumn, fulfilling her duty to Daddy, and looking forward to her upcoming trip to Europe with Lee. Charlie and Martha Bartlett invited her to an informal Sunday supper on Mother's Day, May 13, at their narrow 3419 Q Street residence. They promised her that another guest would be there who they urged she meet, and who Charlie had tried but failed to see earlier in the year. He persevered and "got to be quite a bore about it," Jackie recounted. Charlie Bartlett had attempted to introduce them during his brother David's wedding in 1947, when they were both guests. His friend was war hero, novelist, and Democratic congressman John F. Kennedy, affectionately known as Jack by his family and friends. He met Charlie in 1946 while running for Congress as a Harvard University graduate and a Catholic, and they became close the following year when he was a freshman congressman and Charlie was a Washington newspaper correspondent.

On May 15, two days after the Bartlett dinner, Jackie received a telegram from Vogue's editor in chief, Edna Woolman Chase, saying, "Delighted to announce you have won first prize in Vogue's 16th Prix de Paris." Surprisingly, Jackie took three days to react via telegram: "Can't believe I've won the Prix." I'll be in New York for the entire day on Monday. May I come in and speak with you? I'll call you first thing Monday morning."

Even before Jackie responded to Vogue after winning, Janet joyfully called Betty Beale to have the Washington Star announce her daughter's victory in the Vogue sweepstakes on May 17. Janet's attitude shifted dramatically four days later. Janet had begun a war she intended to win by the time Jackie travelled to New York on May 21 to finish paperwork and make her position at Condé Nast official. When Jackie announced her intention to travel to Paris seven months before, Janet snarled that the only way that could happen was if she won the Vogue contest. Janet was completely opposed to Jackie working for Vogue now that she had officially won.

Janet's steadfast stance was justified for a variety of reasons.

"In Janet's mind, there was something a little undignified about accepting the Vogue prize," said Stephen Birmingham, a biographer of Jackie's who interviewed Janet. It was similar to obtaining a scholarship, which poor people did." Molly Thayer noted that "the family" had "thought it was enough" for her to have already spent a year in Paris. But, in a letter to Vogue on May 7, Jackie stated that she didn't care about returning to Paris; she just wanted "a foot in the door" at Condé Nast. Janet was worried about her six-month stint working for Vogue in New York. Jackie went to meet Black Jack when she travelled to Condé Nast's New York headquarters on May 21 to pose for renowned photographer Richard Routledge and finish her papers. He was allegedly "delighted" by her victory.

She provided the curator of the National Gallery of Art as a character reference on her employment application. She couldn't type and couldn't take shorthand. Her favourite subject to study was literature, while her least favourite was "Sciences, Math." She'd never been bonded, had a home or hospitalisation plan, been a Communist, or agitated for regime overthrow. She didn't have any "Business Experience." Her interests included "riding, theatre, and tennis," while her hobbies included "drawing, making up children's books, collecting ballet books, and photography." Her most recent read was From Here to Eternity, and she devoured Life, Time, the New York Herald Tribune, The Washington Post, The New Yorker, Harper's Bazaar, Atlantic Monthly, and, of course, Vogue on a regular basis. Six days later, Jackie explained in a letter to Mary Campbell on May

27 that she needed to decline the Prix: "I have been discussing it with my mother all week," she wrote, alleging that Mummy still insisted on keeping her "in the home," and talks had "taken all this week to arrive at definite plans."

Jackie and her sister were leaving on their three-month summer trip to Europe, paid for by Mummy and Unk, two weeks and three days after her day at Condé Nast.

"My mother was extremely apprehensive about letting her daughters go alone on such an adventure," Lee Bouvier wrote in their later published travelogue, One Special Summer. "It required a lot of convincing. I talked about the trip as my graduation present for months in advance, and Jackie was dutifully convincing about how well she would care for me and how intelligently she would behave."

Jackie informed Yusha that Janet had threatened to cancel their vacation if she did not agree to forgo the Prix, which would be devastating for her frail sister. Jackie agreed. She would not begin her career at Vogue. Janet had triumphed. So it seemed. If Janet had read Jackie's May 27 letter, she would have discovered that Jackie was still looking for work at the magazine. Jackie devised her own covert plan to appease, then undermine, Mummy.

In her letter, she offered to start at the New York offices in the new year, saying she was "confident" she could "get out of my CIA job," which she had recently committed to start in October. "I'll stay here next fall—I guess to learn to type—and then move to New York in January." I know I'll still want to work for you then—in fact, it's my intention to come in and ask you about a job in January, though I don't think Mummy realises it!"

Jacqueline Bouvier's life had changed dramatically in thirty-five days, bringing with it an understandable spectrum of emotions. She had removed her father from an alcohol rehabilitation centre—and had taken full possession of her car. She had a man on a string who was in love with her, then met one who both delighted and terrified her, with no guarantee of getting to know him well. She was on her way to Europe. She got the job she'd been working for a year for—and then had to turn it down. She discovered how committing to a single objective led to success, but also how easily the best-laid plans could fail. She had pledged a year previously to return to Europe. She wasn't returning to reside, but rather to visit. Jacqueline's graduation from George Washington University on Wednesday, May 30, 1951, appeared almost incidental in the midst of the drama.

Yusha, who was sensitive to every detail, surmised that having to turn down Vogue must have "devastated, then enraged" her, but she "wouldn't have trusted herself to really let her mother know how angry she was." She'd told him eight years before, "Being mad comes and goes so quickly with me." I'm worried I'll hurt someone when I've forgotten how angry I was."

Her go-to response to darker emotions, on the other hand, was humour. "Sometimes a day is so unbelievably awful," she remarked, "that it finally becomes funny"—at least to her. Jackie was overjoyed when pipes burst and flooded Merrywood, destroying some of the chintz furniture Mummy had picked with her decorator Elsie DeWolfe. Jackie's sense of humour was generally shown through practical pranks, but those actions occasionally included a dash of metaphorical ground glass. When Yusha got tired of getting up with her to feed the chickens at Hammersmith, she came over to rub his head with a wet towel drenched in peroxide, turning him shamefully blond. Tucky recalled another occasion when she "accidentally" poured pudding on the lap of a teacher she loathed. Nini, Jackie's stepsister, recounted Jackie sending her to the barn to gather dead chickens, which she subsequently packed elegantly and gave as gifts to nameless "enemies."

One such trick, though, stuck out. This time, Jackie directed Nini to locate a different, specific dead animal near the stables. She

39

delicately wrapped it in a hatbox as a unique gift for someone. Jackie had learned to reply quietly in response to her mother's conduct in order to avoid another frantic outburst and smack. Jacqueline Bouvier, on the other hand, had the ability to strike back with creative statements when the personal breach was so serious. "The whole Vogue thing, not letting her reap the reward of such effort," Vivi Crespi remembered, "that crossed a line, so spiteful."

Jackie had left a wonderful gift for Mummy. The box held a dead snake. Beset by several diseases, the increasingly reclusive Black Jack was overjoyed by Jackie's plan to spend the following six months in New York—Vogue had consented to her delayed start date—before heading for the second half of the Prix in Paris.

Janet was furious when she learned about Jackie's intentions. Her rage was fuelled mostly by the fact that the arrangements jeopardised her goal of getting Jackie properly married, especially after her daughter noted that nearly the entire Vogue staff was female. She began disrupting Jackie's new employment with frantic phone calls, waging an ongoing fight to force her resignation.

Janet's unwavering focus on her daughter's impending marriage began to cloud Jackie's judgement. When she expressed her fear about not meeting a suitable partner during lunch with Vogue's Carol Phillips, the editor described her as "confused and uncertain about her future, a sweet darling girl with not a great deal of confidence." She persuaded her to follow Janet's advice, saying, "Go to Washington, that's where all the boys are."

She had devoted nearly a year of her time and effort to landing the dream job. Her letter to Vogue on May 27 made it obvious that she felt no guilt for deceiving her mother about her intention to take it. Why would she give it up so easily? Her father and her boyfriend were involved in the solution. Jackie could tell for herself that her father had become more withdrawn, beyond his typical possessiveness. It's unclear how much her father spoke about his condition, and he still exuded virility, but his emotional neediness was palpable. Esther Lindstrom, Black Jack's housekeeper, enjoyed gambling with him. He'd take his young lovers out to dinner or to see a show, but none of them were social equals, and he grew tired of them quickly. His nephew Miche and his wife Kath, who were exceptionally kind to him, would later move to New York but were living in South America at the time. While Lee was now in college nearby, she lacked her sister's vibrant chemistry with him. "We all loved him; he was our uncle Jack," Janet's niece Mimi recounted, "but I know he got lonely." He appeared restless in the absence of Jackie, as if nothing truly mattered."

When Jackie told him she was leaving Vogue, he instantly offered her a job in his brokerage firm at the same income as her monthly allowance. Without having to pay rent or other ordinary expenses, and when combined with her allowance, she would have had a monthly income of roughly $1,000, hardly enough to live lavishly but more than double what she had to live within at Merrywood. However, the notion of putting aside whatever creative work she wanted to undertake while also taking on the role of her father's emotional caregiver seemed risky to Jackie. She declined her father's invitation but did everything she could to express her affection for him. According to Lee, "she felt a great responsibility to him in his extreme loneliness."

Black Jack's sadness at the plan's failure was offset by the fact that Jackie would still be visiting New York and living with him, despite the fact that she was purportedly travelling to see John Husted. Seeing both when she was in New York served to hide the purpose of her visits. When they'd last seen one another, in the spring, Jackie and John were dating frequently enough to put an end to Mummy's search for the perfect son-in-law until her daughter returned from Europe. Husted, who fell in love "at first sight," was captivated by her "sensitivity," "originality," and "expression of eternal surprise."

Jackie seems to have grown to appreciate his unwavering loyalty by the fall. "What I hope for you," she wrote to her ex-boyfriend Bev Corbin, "is that the same thing happens to you as quickly and as surely as it did to me." It'll happen when you least expect it." To further persuade herself, she told Corbin that John was not the "sensible boy next door," despite the fact that he was quite traditional. When Jackie returned to Merrywood in the fall of 1951, she was riding her horse Sagebrush unusually hard and was thrown from her steed and knocked unconscious. Black Jack reminded her that she'd broken her collarbone and acquired a pinched nerve in her neck from prior incidents, and he threatened to cut off her allowance if she didn't stop riding. She didn't stop, and he didn't cut her off. Her father's diminished control over her was highlighted by a rare but critical move made on her behalf by her stepfather.

Unk and Mummy were still mocked by Black Jack as "Uncle Toady the Naval Hero and your Goddamn Mother," but in the almost a dozen years since he'd been Jackie's stepfather, Unk had earned her trust, and finally her love. He stopped Janet's attacks on her daughter from escalating on multiple occasions. Jackie modelled his unyielding, often distant calm. While Janet was successful in convincing Jackie to leave New York, Yusha believed it had "only made her more determined to work in the writing field." Unk, who seemed to value her ambition more than his wife, intervened. He asked if he might share some of her stories and drawings with his buddy, New York Times Washington bureau chief Arthur Krock, who had a history of assisting smart or well-connected young women in pursuing journalism careers. Krock subsequently told writer Dorothy McCardle that after reading "some of her writing and [seeing] sketches," he called his old friend Frank C. Waldrop, executive editor of the Washington Times-Herald, and added, "Jackie was smart in school too."

"Are you still hiring little girls?" In his October 1951 phone contact, Krock inquired about Jackie Bouvier. "Well, I've got one for you. What can you do with the greatest one—round-eyed, clever—who wants to go into journalism?"

Waldrop directed Krock to his office. Waldrop, a forty-six-year-old father of three, was a dedicated journalist. He grew up in Alabama, attended West Point and Columbia, and began working as a reporter for the Nashville Tennessean the year Jackie was born, at the age of twenty-four, eventually becoming an editorial writer, editorial page editor, managing editor, and political editor. He moved to Washington in 1933 to work for the Washington Herald, which was owned by William Randolph Hearst. Hearst sold it, along with the Washington Times, to Cissy Patterson of the McCormick-Medill publishing family in 1939. Patterson died three years before Jackie arrived, and the merged Washington Times-Herald paper was sold to her cousin Robert McCormick. It had the greatest circulation in the city, with 10 daily issues.

The enterprise occupied four levels in the old Herald Building downtown, two blocks north and three blocks east of the White House, at 1307 H Street. The newsroom was on the ground floor, with windows that faced the street. As executive editor, Waldrop had a big glassed-in office here, which Jackie first visited in early October 1951. Initially, Waldrop said she "mumbled around saying something about pictures," referring to photography. "Do you really want to go into journalism or do you want to hang around here until you get married?" he questioned simply.

"No, sir," Jackie answered. "I want to make a career."

"I'll be serious if you're serious." If not, you can work clipping things."

"No, sir. "I'm not kidding."

"I don't want you to come back here in six months and say you're engaged."

Waldrop's well-honed account, reiterated in nearly a dozen interviews over thirty years, muddled the precise date or concealed seemingly trivial facts that were ultimately necessary in outlining the complete arc of Jackie's journalistic career from that moment forward. He most likely did so as an act of loyalty, in collaboration with her; the fuller version made her drive more admirable, but when her story was first told, she didn't want to be cast as ruthlessly ambitious, nor did she want it revealed that she had started on the clerical staff rather than the reporting staff.

According to a congratulatory message she received from Mary Campbell at Vogue, Jackie started working at the Times-Herald on Monday, October 15, 1951. She began with a sense of entitlement but rapidly realised that, despite having a billionaire stepfather, she still had to prove herself. She started as a "gofer," getting coffee for the clerical workers and working as a receptionist at the front desk. "I didn't care how well she'd written in school; she wasn't going to be hired as a reporter," Waldrop explained. I'd seen her before. Little society girls who want to write the great American novel but give up the moment they find the great American husband."

When he realised "they were serious," he promoted them "as secretaries to acquire the feel of the place—get familiar and see what they could do.... They actually answered my phone.... It piqued my interest. "How would these girls fit in at the newspaper?"

By week two, Jackie Bouvier was using "persistent charm" to remind Waldrop that she was there to write and was eager to use her talent for any dull task he saw fit. "She had the ability to look around corners. "She sat down and got to work," he recounted. "I've never complained about secretary duties." She couldn't type 'cat,' yet she managed to... bore me down."

By the third week, he had appointed Jackie as his personal assistant. "I did request that she write some routine letters for me, but she couldn't take dictation or type, so it wasn't worth the time." I was just having her answer the phone and take messages. Thorough. I asked a dozen questions to everyone who called... self-sufficient, adept at listening, and efficient."

As word spread that Waldrop's new aide was the former Deb of the Year, she became something of a novelty in the newsroom, especially because she was ecstatic to be working for the publication. "I never imagined a millionaire's daughter could be so cocky as to take a low-paying job like this," one colleague remarked.

On the last day of October, she took advantage of her opportunity. Princess Elizabeth of England, twenty-five, arrived at National Airport from Montreal wearing a fabric coat with two diamond lapel pins in the shape of the Canadian maple leaf, escorted by her husband, Philip, Duke of Edinburgh. The motorcade began its four-mile drive into Washington with the open lead car carrying the princess and President Harry S. Truman, followed by the prince, First Lady Bess Truman, and the Trumans' daughter, Margaret, to roaring cheers from the half-million citizens on the sidewalks. Jackie was one of many who pushed forward in the hopes of catching a glimpse of the princess. Mr. Waldrop had allowed her to go down and observe everything. She regarded it as an opportunity to demonstrate her abilities as a journalist.

The first event on Elizabeth's hectic three-day itinerary was an invitation-only press gathering at the Statler Hotel, where almost a thousand reporters crammed into the ballroom, including Mummy's friend Betty Beale, the Washington Evening Star's society columnist. "I know everyone in town, and I've known Jackie since she was a teenager, and I saw that right in the middle of all the invited press was Jackie," Beale explained. "She had no place there." She was not a member of the press. She worked as a secretary! Jackie is the one! She pushes to achieve what she wants and disregards rules when they do not suit her. She must have sneaked in and said she worked for the paper—without mentioning that she was filing papers and sending communications! Oh, she was the one!"

Waldrop remembered Jackie returning to the workplace with a handwritten, funny essay full of quotes demonstrating how enamoured government workers cheering on the sidewalks were with a monarch. "I told her I wouldn't be able to use it. She was taken aback. 'You're not a reporter!' I said. And she lowered her head... 'Oh... Mr. Waldrop. "I'm truly sorry." But her attempt inspired Waldrop. There was a young man working as a freelance "stringer" for the daily (his identity was never disclosed) who wrote the "Inquiring Photographer" section—a feature familiar to readers since the publication was simply "the Herald." The column, which was published six days a week, comprised comments from a half-dozen random people to the same subject, as well as their names and images, which required the columnist to photograph them with a big Speed Graflex. In narrative form, Jackie's story had virtually done the same thing. Waldrop instructed her to accompany the stringer and listen, then to formulate her own question regarding Elizabeth's visit and ask it to whomever she desired. Waldrop would then choose which to include in the following day's column.

Jackie Bouvier's debut piece appeared in the Times-Herald on November 2, 1951, with the query "Is Princess Elizabeth as pretty as her picture?" She questioned six Times-Herald staff photographers: Berkeley Payne, Byrd Ferneyhough, William Luers, James Zimmerman, Wellner Streets, and W. Paul Dennehy. It was unique and flattering for the faces that were always behind the camera to stand in front of it—and tactically astute on Jackie's part.

The paper had a history of publishing a disproportionate number of female columnists. Waldrop, who edited them all, discovered that they were best when "able to tell things in very concise short terms." The timing was also impeccable. "I knew I needed a new Inquiring Photographer—the kid doing it was a stringer who was quitting to go to law school," Waldrop recounted. The issue was that no one sought the position. "We used to make jokes about being in the dog house when we were assigned to the Inquiring Photographer spot," one reporter remembered. "They would rather sit in a bar than take mugshots of people standing on street corners answering stupid questions." Nobody could imagine someone liking the job and volunteering to not only pose the questions but also snap the photographs." In truth, the "Inquiring Photographer" never had a byline since the columnists were constantly changing; no one did it frequently enough to claim it as their own.

"I'll tell you what we'll do," Waldrop said. "You can try out for this thing." He urged her to continue going out with the stringer, but to ask her own questions once a week and submit the answers on a trial basis. Jackie realised she could do something unique with the "Inquiring Photographer" feature that no one else desired at the paper. On November 9, for what was likely her next published column, Jackie asked a question that demonstrated it might serve as an outlet for all she was thinking at the time: "Should a girl live at home until she gets married, or go out to see how it is to live alone?"

Jackie was debating if she could afford to rent her own apartment at the time. Jackie Bouvier was employed for a weekly salary of $25 (about $270 in today's currencies), according to managing editor Sidney Epstein. She spent a large portion of it on her twice-monthly train or plane tickets to see John Husted in New York, the gas to drive Zelda from McLean, Virginia, to downtown D.C. five times a week, and parking in a covered garage rather than fighting for an open space on the streets, as the other employees did. She'd have little additional money if she rented her own place, but that wasn't the only reason she hesitated. She was desperate to get away from Merrywood, where there was an increase in the maternal whining about her need to find the appropriate husband. Nonetheless, a single woman living on her own was looked down on, at least by the traditions of her class. Her nervousness about breaking such a taboo was reflected in the question she posed for the piece.

Of the five women and one man she asked, four essentially said it really depended on the individual. Mrs. R. W. Bradley, however, seemed to best speak to Jackie's dilemma. A girl should stay home until married, she said, but "go out and have a good time, meet boys, and go to… dances and nightclubs."

That column brought an epiphany. Jackie Bouvier knew not to seek advice from Black Jack or Mummy; each would respond in a way that favoured him- or herself and disparaged the other. She could correspond with Yusha or Father Leonard, but their response would be delayed by mail. Seeking advice from a diverse demographic of strangers who had neither a vested interest in her choice nor knowledge that the questions might be about her personal life could help clarify whatever concerned her. It was an early sign of what became a defining characteristic of Jackie's as an adult, being simultaneously overt and covert. Jackie went to see John Husted in New York on the weekend of November 10. While there, he took her home to Bedford Hills to meet his doting mother. When Helen Husted pulled out his baby picture to give her as a gift, Jackie recoiled, insisting she could take her own photo of him. She would later tell a friend how John "adored mama maybe a bit too much," and found it "weird how he praised her as this ideal, old-fashioned wife." For her next trial column, on November 14, her question sarcastically referenced what John seemed to want from her: "Is it possible to now find a girl like the one who married dear old dad?"

Her column published on November 23 perhaps reflected an uncertainty about her skill for the job ("What is the silliest question anyone ever asked you?"), but also revealed her already artful efforts to make it compelling. She targeted some switchboard operators who'd never been asked such a question and chose unpredictable responses. Olive Frazier answered that she'd once been asked by a caller for the day, year, time, and location, joking, "She really must have been mixed up—or well mixed." Shorty Shipe was angry at being repeatedly asked why he seemed to be a sociopathic liar ("I get a kick out of it."). Pauline Stafford was befuddled when asked to explain the difference between a horse and a mule. Joe Mercillott got defensive about being asked why he flipped an auto while driving ("I didn't turn the car over deliberately.").

Jackie spent Thanksgiving weekend with the Auchinclosses at Merrywood, then went to New York to see Black Jack and John. Typically, Jackie responded to unwelcome and excessive declarations of romantic love with, as John recalled, her "devastating, cutting wit." That only seemed to make him fall deeper in love; what he saw as her "very good sense of humour" was a primary quality that kept him besotted.

As if it were part of the approaching holiday season's festivities, John now sprang a cheeky dare on her. Based on his presumption that they "had sort of declared our love for each other," he suggested she "prove it" by marrying him. Before she could say anything, however, he made a game of it. She would be returning to New York the weekend before Christmas to exchange gifts with her father. "I told her to meet me at the Polo Bar of the Westbury Hotel at noon on [that] Saturday," where she could "tell me your answer." She was grateful to be spared any expectation of an immediate reply to his proposition, since she seemed unable to muster inspiration for sharing her life with him. He just wasn't the man she had imagined marrying.

The questions she had to pose in order to write her column now served as a way to learn how others felt about her ambivalence. On December 6 she posed her most highly personal question yet: "Should a girl pass up sound matrimonial prospects to wait for her ideal man?" Of the five people questioned, only one advised holding out. Eleven days later, on the seventeenth, her uncertainty remained as she asked six servicemen, "What was the closest you've ever come to being enticed into matrimony?" Five were relieved to be single and one admitted he'd married "in a weak moment."

When Waldrop asked to see Jackie, she was going to leave to see her father, then return to Merrywood to enjoy Christmas with the Auchinclosses, and eventually travel with them to Florida, where they would stay until the new year. He advised her to "come back after the first of the year," when he'd make a final decision on

49

whether to hire her as a permanent writer. Her marriage-related concerns may have raised his suspicions, and he reminded her of his caution during their initial discussion in October. "Don't come back if you're just passing the time until you get engaged!"

"Being a journalist seemed the ideal way of both having a job and experiencing the world, especially for anyone with a sense of adventure," she would explain years later to Gloria Steinem. "Journalism offers variety.... Being a reporter appears to be a ticket out of the world."

However, her persistence in pestering Waldrop about a writing job until she went for the holiday caused him to snap. "She became quiet and looked down... but she was thinking." I inquired if she was familiar with the paper's departments and beats—the courts, theatre, and crime. 'What interests you enough to do it day in and out, Miss Bouvier?!' ""She looked up, right into my eyes, and said, 'Everything.'"

Then she appeared to throw it all aside.

CHAPTER 7

PALM BEACH

On the Saturday before Christmas, it was snowing fiercely. Jackie's train was delayed arriving in New York, so she wasn't sure whether she'd still be able to meet John at the Westbury Hotel, but she told the cab driver to take her up to Madison Avenue and 69th Street anyhow.

The tall Yalie, bruised but not surprised, had been sitting inside the hotel's Polo Bar by himself since lunchtime and was going to pay his bill and leave. Jackie Bouvier "breezed in," stepped up to his table, and simply replied, "Yes." According to John Husted, she appeared to be accepting a dare rather than joyfully taking the first step toward sharing her life with someone she loved at the time.

They hurried over to Black Jack's apartment. John had seen him once previously, in the late 1940s, when he and Jackie competed in a father-daughter tennis tournament at Miss Porter's. As the first to learn of their news, he was overjoyed not because his daughter was married, but because she would be relocating to New York. John asked him for his daughter's hand in marriage with customary decorum. The polite John Husted was perplexed by the old man's response: "Sure—but it will never work."

Neither Black Jack nor Jackie explained his strange comment.

Soon after, she wrote to Father Leonard that she was "terribly in love—for the first time—and I want to marry." And I KNOW I'm going to marry this boy. I don't have to ponder if they're the right one, how we'd get along, and so on, like I used to. I just KNOW he is, and it's the most wonderful sensation in the world."

Jackie sensed Mummy's confusion when she joined her family for Christmas a few days later. She had agreed to her dating John at first. During the preceding months, she'd accepted him as a potential son-in-law, making no effort to steer her daughter toward another potential suitor. Yusha reported that when Jackie accepted John's proposal, Janet darkly remarked that it was because her daughter was knocked unconscious when she was tossed from Sagebrush. It all felt a little too simple.

Janet's growing dissatisfaction with the marriage could be related to her revelation that John Husted's net worth and salary fell short of her expectations. Mummy had thus ended up with the polar opposite of what she had desired: an insufficiently wealthy husband for Jackie who resided in the same city as her ex-husband. Lee reasoned that Janet's disapproval fostered Jackie's passive drive to oppose her, but it's difficult to envision her sacrificing her happiness merely to anger her mother. The fact that she was "extremely anxious to leave home" appears to be the more valid explanation. She may have been affected by Janet's frightening projections that she was on the verge of a lonely, destitute future as a single woman for which professional fulfilment could never compensate; that she needed to seize a likely last chance to guarantee a comfortable future.

However, Waldrop's threat that if she became engaged, he would not hire her as a columnist was not part of the sexist postwar belief that a married woman should not work on the assumption that her husband earned enough to support her, or that her holding the job prevented a man from having it and earning an income. There were a lot of married women writers at the Times-Herald, and Waldrop simply didn't want to put in the effort to train her if she was going to depart shortly. John Husted never forced Jackie to quit her job, but travelling to New York with him after marriage would preclude her from working at the Washington Post.

Jackie was different from most girls her age because she believed she might make her own money, possibly a substantial one, by becoming a famous writer. She appeared to be alone in this, bolstered by Bernard Berenson's advice that working in a job one enjoys was the way to happiness. John Husted had set a deadline for her response to his marriage proposal, and she still didn't know if she'd be recruited as a columnist. She might have felt she had no choice but to marry.

Another reason that has mostly gone unnoticed is a better explanation for her decision, considering what she said at the time about her excitement—but also self-doubt—about being the "Inquiring Photographer" columnist. If she ignored Waldrop's unequivocal warning that she would be fired if she were engaged, Jackie would have an excuse for why she wasn't employed. It would be a shield for her ego, but it would mean giving up her best shot of becoming a professional writer. When Carol Phillips of Vogue interviewed Jackie three months previously about her position as a junior editor, she had "not a great deal of confidence." The same uncertainty could be seen later in her fear of pursuing an artistic profession, as she told a friend at his photography exhibit, "I wish I could do what you're doing—but I can't." A strong insecurity about her capacity to be recruited and keep the job could be the reason she decided to defy social norms and get engaged.

A BALMY FLORIDA VACATION promised to distract Jackie from the uncomfortable uncertainty she was experiencing. After Christmas, the Auchincloss family visited Unk's cousins in the exclusive town of Hobe Sound.

Charlie and Martha Bartlett were visiting his parents in Hobe Sound. Charlie, it appears, persuaded the Bouvier sisters to accompany him on a day trip to Palm Beach to see friends, the Kennedys. He may have done so on purpose. "Jackie was engaged to a fellow whom we didn't think much of," he recounted. "He was a nice fellow, but he didn't seem to be worthy of her hand."

One entered the high white stucco wall at 1095 North Ocean Boulevard via a large wood door reminiscent of castle drawbridges.

Jackie and her friends entered and strolled down a covered colonnade overlooking tennis courts. Inside was a buzzing hive where guests were expected to compete in displays of athletic prowess, razor-sharp wit, and current events and world history knowledge.

A touch football game on the emerald lawn beyond the home frequently featured all of Ambassador Kennedy's active and gorgeous adult children. Jackie knew some of them, though the specifics of how and when are unknown. She was already acquainted with the "star" of the family, Jack, whom the Bartletts had "shamelessly matchmaking." The two hadn't spoken since May, when Jackie had declined his invitation to join him for a drink after dinner at the Bartletts', but she might have seen him recently—on national television. In the ensuing months, both of their lives had taken unforeseen turns.

Eunice, a Stanford University graduate who had been working as a social worker in Washington when Jackie started at GWU, was among Jack's siblings who had gathered for the holidays. (Her earliest memory of Jackie was that she was a tennis player who also knew French and did "both well.") Jackie and Bobby's wife, Ethel, had met through mutual friends, most likely the Bartletts. Bobby, who was only twenty-five years old at the time, was a Justice Department criminal division lawyer and the father of a five-month-old daughter named Kathleen. There were also television producers Pat (27), Jean (23), and Teddy (19) on leave from basic training. Typically, the events featured their prep school and college pals, as well as Jack's naval friends. The Ambassador's activities, according to Charlie, centred around the "swimming pool, movies, tennis courts, family games, lunch [on the] patio." When they met for lunch at the stone-floored courtyard's white wrought-iron tables and chairs, the conversation was mostly light, punctuated by joking, needling, and one-upping about the morning's competitions, but it also featured serious discussion of current issues.

The 1951 Christmas was the family's first time together since the summer. Eunice and Jean had just returned from a trip to the Mediterranean and the Middle East. Eunice, who was focused on political issues, told the Boston Post that the United States' sustained backing for Greece's monarchy was a role in keeping it as a Cold War ally, as "the nation's one stabilising permanent influence." Jack had visited England, Germany, France, and Australia earlier in the year, but the seven weeks he spent with Bobby and Pat in Israel, Iran, Pakistan, India, Singapore, Thailand, Vietnam, Korea, and Japan from October 7 to November 30 changed him—and perhaps the prospects for his political rise. Kennedy had been determined since entering Congress, training to become a foreign-relations expert, and home pictures showing the trio at the Taj Mahal and the Bangkok shopping area belied the political purpose of their visits. Jack spoke with the leaders of each country, learning about the dangers of Iran falling under Soviet control unless oil revenues were restored, India's need for US food help, and developing anti-Americanism in Pakistan. Just before Pakistani Prime Minister Liaquat Ali Khan was assassinated in October, he penned a Boston Post report about his interview with him.

The lawmaker was determined to reshape America's Cold War foreign policy. He identified the dots between US foreign aid and gaining nonaligned developing nations as allies before the Communist Soviet Union and China, but not simply to boost American global domination. He was also committed to raise the individuals with whom he had worked out of poverty. In an era when most US officials travelled abroad only to glamorous European capitals, the journey blasted open his understanding of world politics. Vietnam piqued his interest the most. On October 19, the three Kennedys landed in Saigon, when Jack angrily questioned the soundness of their entire military strategy, infuriating both the French general and an American Embassy official.

Jack's deathly illness, with a fever of 106 degrees, during their final trip in Japan, where he was hospitalised on Okinawa (he had neglected to take medication that helped keep his adrenal-gland insufficiency under control), was barely noted in media accounts. Instead of resting, Jack engaged in an intense public speaking schedule from the moment he returned until he hit Palm Beach, blending charm and knowledge before crowds that might have gathered for cosy tales of his famous family but came away learning about the far reaches of the world, from the Pittsfield Chamber of Commerce to the Lowell Service Club to the Framingham Catholic Women's Club. He covered foreign aid and Cold War policies using just a map to depict his itinerary and extemporaneous recall of detailed details from his trip notes.

On December 1, he made an appearance on the national news show Meet the Press. His criticism of US Embassy officials for being more interested in "tennis games and cocktail parties" than learning about the challenges confronting the people of their host countries made headlines, but his appraisal of the situation in Vietnam was more crucial. He suggested that the US should not continue to provide strong military support to the French against the North Vietnamese guerrillas, who were backed by Chinese Communists and sought control of Vietnam. Instead, it must persuade France to surrender its colonial control over that nation and allow it to become self-governing and autonomous. According to Kennedy, the Vietnamese aspired to independence and increasingly saw the American relationship with France as aiding the continuation of their domination. He concluded that the implications of not changing policy would be Communist China's eventual dominance in the country. His November 15 radio address, which was nationally syndicated by the Mutual Broadcasting System, succinctly articulated his observation that Vietnam, Cambodia, and Laos, as "French principalities," were "as typical examples of empire and colonialism as can be found anywhere," and that the United States' role in ignoring their "nationalistic aims spells foredoomed failure."

Thus, the Jack whom Jackie met at the end of 1951 was different from the carefree flirt she'd met seven months earlier at the Bartletts', in May. He was intense. He was serious. He was in perpetual motion. He sought out General MacArthur to confer on classified Korean War developments. More nationalistic than partisan, he defied President Truman, lobbying him to revise his peace treaty with Italy and permit the country into the United Nations. As columnist David Rudsten observed in a June 1, 1951, editorial, "In the field of foreign politics [Kennedy] early recognized our weakness through disarmament and urged larger expenditures for national defence," developing "a liberal foreign policy that recognizes America's leading position and responsibility in world affairs." The congressman had also "studied federal legislation procedures quietly and efficiently," and "his efforts on behalf of education, labour and veteran's housing won him wide recognition."

Despite his play for national attention on foreign affairs, Jack paid assiduous mind to every matter affecting Massachusetts. Instead of using congressional breaks to relax, Kennedy spent hours every day of the week each summer and fall visiting the cities and towns of the Bay State, speaking before any civic organisation that would invite him.

His high profile in the state caused some to speculate that he wanted to become governor, but his intent was to challenge the popular Republican U.S. senator Henry Cabot Lodge. As Kennedy had calculated, becoming senator was a necessary step to becoming president of the United States.

"He really wasn't normal—he had a drive, and intense interest in everything," noted businessman Lemoyne "Lem" Billings, Jack's best friend and confidant since their Choate days. His "brightness" had always been there, revealed less by his school grades than by his curiosity and reading habits. Even as a teenager, Billings noticed, Jack "read the New York Times every day."

That "interest in everything," Vietnam included, also characterised Jackie Bouvier—Kennedy's observations about his time there would have drawn her curiosity. She knew the French colonial attitude well, even if her own views on it hadn't fully formed. Years later, Teddy

Kennedy offered that, on that day Jackie visited, Jack surely discussed Vietnam, "since it was so much on his mind right after that trip," and recalled as well the fact that she "had a long history of interest in the conflict there," speculating that it was likely they "would talk about it."

Jackie was also immediately impressed by the powerful Ambassador, a fact putting her at odds with both Black Jack and Gramps Lee, who were united in their hatred of him. As Securities and Exchange Commission chairman, Joe Kennedy's crackdown on specialist stock brokerage commissions resulted in Black Jack's catastrophic 1936 decline. The year Jackie was born, according to Jack Davis, Jim Lee and Joe Kennedy had been such good friends that the former told the latter he was about to make a lucrative investment in a piece of Chicago real estate known as the Merchandise Mart, then the world's largest building, with four million square feet of retail space. Kennedy acted fast and bought it himself. Being "double-crossed" like that caused Lee to have "eternal enmity" for Kennedy.

Despite the outrage it would cause her father and grandfather—or perhaps because of it—Jackie was unrepentant in later declaring that of the entire family, Joe was her "most adored." The feeling became mutual quickly. "Papa Kennedy," recalled Charlie Bartlett, "thought she was great." In time she would learn of his unsavoury business manoeuvres, antisemitism, and manipulation of the media and political system to benefit Jack, but she turned a blind eye to these. "I am sick of all the mean stories of old Joe," she would later tell a friend. "No one knows the great heart that man has." This may well be how she felt about him, but it also showed her opportunism—even if it didn't work out with Jack, having Ambassador Kennedy as a friend could prove useful in her professional ambitions. Jackie didn't meet Jack's mother when she first visited. "The first I ever heard of Jackie was sometime during the winter of 1951," Rose Fitzgerald Kennedy would write, noting that Jackie was working at the paper. When she soon after received a thank-you note signed "Jackie," she recalled wondering, "[W]ho is Jackie?" She would come to know the answer soon.

PART 5

"Would you rather have men respect you or whistle at you?"

—JACKIE, IN HER "INQUIRING PHOTOGRAPHER" COLUMN

CHAPTER 8

THE BLUE ROOM

With the lively, worldly Kennedy household fresh in her mind, Jackie stepped confidently into Waldrop's office "the first week of January," braced for his certain rage at her breaching her commitment not to marry. Their discussion, as Waldrop described it in two later interviews, demonstrated him to be a colourful storyteller.

"Well, I'm sorry," she stated emphatically, "but I can't take the job."

"Why not?!" Waldrop remembered snapping at her, "a bit angry."

"I got engaged over Christmas."

Her candour had an unexpected result. "I've always liked her for doing this because it was an honourable thing to do," Waldrop added. He also admired her "straightforward manner in dealing with me." She informed him she'd only known her fiancé, John Husted, for a short time.

"It won't last," he assuredly said. "Get out there and go to work."

Hers was a masterful use of reverse psychology. Waldrop had not yet officially offered her the columnist position, but by unexpectedly proclaiming herself ineligible, she persuaded him that she should continue her training.

While satisfied with her trial columns, Waldrop was hesitant to hire her since "these bastards in the photographic department were all going out and taking the pictures for her."

"I'm also a photographer, and I used a Leica at the Sorbonne," Jackie assured managing editor Sidney Epstein. He burst out laughing. "We don't have anything that fancy here, kid; you'll use a Speed Graflex." When he handed her the enormous, clunky camera for the first time, he noted her "puzzled, worried look." He gave her a day to figure things out.

"She didn't know one end of a camera from the other when she came to us," Waldrop jokes. Her "pictures were awful." Several staff photographers were determined to educate her the proper distance to stand at in order to acquire clear thumbnail shots of her interviewees, close enough to capture detail while remaining clear. It wasn't enough to take shots from the proper distance; she also had to handle the Graflex and the large, circular flash that was attached to it. She looked up the Scurlock Studio's Capitol School of Photography on the second floor of 1813 Eighteenth Street in the Yellow Pages and joined up for intensive, accelerated training. "She was smart," Waldrop subsequently told reporter Dorothy McCardle. She picked up quickly.``

Although Jackie's attendance at a photography school was highlighted in her later bios, the one she selected to attend revealed something about her progressive ideas on racial integration. Addison Scurlock, well-known for documenting Washington's African American society, founded the studio in 1911, and his son, Robert, a former Tuskegee airman, founded the school in 1948. He was a Graflex master and a photojournalist whose work appeared in national periodicals. African Americans on the G.I. Bill was among Jackie's classmates. It also welcomed women, stating in its brochure that they had "exceptional skill in Child Photography, Fashion Work, Retouching, and Oil Colouring."

Photojournalist George Thames, who later worked for the New York Times, heard "many amusing stories" about Jackie from the newspaper's staff photographers, who struck an instant bond with her. "The first time one of her photos appeared in her column, the other photographers said, 'You should buy us a drink,' so she went out and bought a quart of milk to tease these guys."

"[S]he had her own ideas about what made the best picture," Thames said, but she was frustrated by her failure to get outstanding photographs. In expressing gratitude to a friend for a "beautiful coloured picture," Jackie stated, "you are a fantastic photographer—which makes me very jealous." She would have a lifelong admiration for the work of the female photographers she met, such as Berenice Abbott, Lily Emmet Cushing, and Toni Frissell. Jackie's hunt for the most diverse content took her well outside her wealthy comfort zone. Waldrop, who was invested in her success, took her "on a brief tour of police and hospital spots to get a look at the life of the city." She strolled through hotel lobbies, dove in and out of taxis and city buses, popped into neighbourhood stores, and lingered outside office buildings and government agencies, interacting with bureaucrats and clerical, service, and domestic workers and becoming acquainted with their lives.

Despite her engagement, Jackie was named the "Inquiring Photographer" writer on Monday, January 21, 1952. Her initial income was roughly doubled, to $42.50 per week (about $500 in today's currencies, the annual equivalent of $19,656). "The column improved immediately," Waldrop stated. "She was shy and soft-spoken, but she wasn't afraid to go out on the street and get her columns." I imagine the previous youngster would go into a pub and interview the first five individuals he encountered." Waldrop valued her insight into human nature more than her camera talents. "Everything is dependent on how well the interview was handled—not the picture," Waldrop explained. "She had no idea how to take images. But she knew how to approach people."

The dreaded newspaper announcement of her engagement to John Husted arrived on the same day, though Waldrop discouraged her from thinking she would have to give up her career in six months to become a stockbroker's bride, never believing she would go through with it. Indeed, their engagement party at Merrywood became infamous for its bleak tone. Sherry Geyelin, the daughter of Unk's brokerage partner Chauncey Parker III, described the weather as "cold... no warmth there." Mummy's rage flared when John's aunt Helen moved some flowers, resulting in an argument. Jackie revealed to Unk's distant relative, author Louis Auchincloss, that she was depressed about the inevitably "peaceful but dull" life that becoming Mrs. John Husted promised.

Her new career quickly absorbed more of her attention and inspired more pride than her engagement. Jackie arrived with gloves on during a meeting with her friend Mary de Limur, who knew Husted, but removed the left one to show her the engagement ring, which had belonged to John's mother. Jackie stated that the green discoloration on De Lima's fingernails was caused by the chemicals she used to develop her column images. "She immediately launched into a lengthy and detailed description of her job at the newspaper." "She just kept going," de Limur remembered. "Finally, almost as an afterthought, she stated that they had planned to marry in June... She appeared unconcerned about it."

Jackie was out on her patrol when she received a plea for help. The newsroom was abuzz as soon as the caller's name and phone number were left. When she returned, Waldrop had already delivered her message, along with a sarcastic admonition to "stay away from the guy if she wanted to avoid trouble." He knew the caller well, but it wasn't his reputation that made him hesitate: it was concern for what going out with other men may do to the reputation of a newly engaged woman. It was Congressman Kennedy who invited her to the dinner and orchestra dance at the Shoreham Hotel's Blue Room on most evenings.

When she arrived for dinner, she was greeted by two men: Jack had brought along his Boston ally Dave Powers, who would later help design Kennedy's Senate campaign strategy. It's unlikely he invited Dave to accompany them as a chaperone; Jack Kennedy was unconcerned with polite society's rules. Even if he hadn't heard about her engagement through Jackie during her Palm Beach vacation, the news had broken before their supper. Jackie was unlikely to pursue a man who was not interested in dating, as she had suspected of Jack when they first met, but she was intrigued enough by his motives to accept. She didn't think it was wrong to go out with a single man even though she was engaged.

Although Jackie remembered it as the "first time I went out with him," and their intention was "to dance," the moment she saw Jack's "political friend from Boston," as well as crutches to relieve his back pain from compressed nerves (the result of a war injury), it was clear that it was more of a meeting than a night of romantic dancing. The Blue Room's "Supper Dance" featured an eight-course meal that included everything from celery and olives to after-dinner cordials. There would be no disruptions because the hotel did "not page in the Blue Room." Dinner was provided till ten o'clock, with a choice of broiled bluefish, capon breast, roast lamb, cold ham, turkey, or beef, served with potatoes, with Jackie usually opting for something light and Jack invariably preferring red meat. They probably found their shared love of ice cream over bowls of "Shoreham Desire." They most likely left before the Barnee-Lowe Orchestra floor show because of their early work hours.

Given that, while Congress was in session, there were some weeks when Jack Kennedy would fly north and take the sleeper train back to Washington for a day of work (during which he liked to challenge himself by reading an entire book), he had to be extremely motivated to arrange seeing Jackie Bouvier. In late January and early February, he was also touring the Bay State, making a half-dozen appearances from Springfield to Pittsfield to the Berkshires.

Most people felt Kennedy's attempt to topple Lodge was merely a publicity stunt, but he enjoyed the almost impossible endeavour. "There wouldn't be much enjoyment in life without an obstacle," his close friend and investment banker Chuck Spalding observed. The possible competition "was one hurdle... [he] enjoyed, talked about, and laughed about."

"He had the wealth, the education, the political acumen," said Massachusetts politician Wilton Vaughn, but "perseverance more than anything else" defined him. His colleague in Congress, Olin Teague, was struck by his determination and how "he was very much his own boss." He had extremely favourable thoughts about what was good and bad for this country... and he wasn't afraid to share them... Jack worked really hard in his studies.... He was concentrating on informing himself... He was a self-sufficient individual who was intellectually fully honest."

He didn't appear or act like a millionaire. His ill-fitting suits and wrinkled shirts marked him as a man in need of the kind of wardrobe advice Jackie had discussed in her Vogue essay; however, if seeing the family's Palm Beach mansion wasn't enough evidence, a January news story about his sister Jean's jewellery being stolen, with the disclosure that it was valued at $357,000, made the family's staggering wealth clear.

His laid-back manner belied his cunning desire. As a Harvard student before his first congressional campaign, Jack even had his own driver and valet, George Taylor, an African American Cambridge resident who knew the local "bigwigs" well. Taylor testified that after graduating in 1940, Jack Kennedy intended to pursue a political career and asked him to "introduce me to all the politicians in this area," contradicting the popular myth that his father persuaded Jack to run for office after the death of his older brother, Joe, for whom Joe Senior had harboured similar ambitions. "I've never seen anyone so engulfed," Taylor remarked. "He just loved it—he talked about politics all the time."

Taylor noted that Jack had started by looking up one man: "He'd always look up Dave Powers to get information as to the possibilities of what was in store for him in the future." The precinct worker from

Boston's working-class Charleston neighbourhood had befriended Jack and helped him win three successive congressional campaigns since 1946. Powers possessed a legendary recall as well as "recognized talent and people who were able to get things done," according to Kennedy biographer Terry Golway. Powers was now planning a campaign strategy for Jack's potential challenge to Lodge.

Jackie left no record of her first impressions of Powers, but he was immediately impressed, he said, by her "intelligence and utterly original insights," and recognized an "iron determination when she saw something could be achieved."

Jackie recalled that Powers had been "rather left out of the conversation," but told by Jack that she was Republican "old society," Powers hoped she might offer "insight" into how Lodge, from the same milieu, might respond to political attacks intended to break what political columnist Mary McGrory called his "bland adroitness." Her family didn't know Lodge, and she didn't tell Powers anything he didn't know, but he found her observation and suggestions of help she could provide unexpected: "Jackie is a perfectionist; anything she did, she wanted to do very well—and she became very, very good at it. That went to politics, too."

She realised that her aptitude for languages could help Kennedy with the mail that came into the Boston office from Massachusetts Italian, French, and Spanish speakers. "I was shocked that she knew there were many French Canadians in the old mill cities Lawrence and Lowell," Powers recalled.

"I have never met anyone like her," Jack would tell Dave Powers in good time, "she's different from any girl I know."

CHAPTER 9

OUT ON THE STREET

Her desk was a shambles. She was sitting on top of it, pecking out her bundle of daily quotes, a tiresome activity for someone inexperienced as a typist and used to handwritten everything. Around the machine, there was a mess of pencils and pads. According to Waldrop, she was evidently too preoccupied with making her daily deadline to care about keeping her desk tidy. "She focussed on the day's question. "She paid close attention," he stated. "She treated it as a small business, but it was significant enough to launch her writing career." She was simply solemn." Larry Jacobs, a picture editor, shared her workstation, where she placed interview transcripts for future columns, bits of factual research, or provocative quotations for future queries in a bottom drawer. He remembered it as "pretty full" and "looking much as though a recent hurricane had hit it a good deal of the time."

She lured an acquaintance and NBC Radio staffer, Everette Severe, whom she also interviewed, back to her office one day when she was running late for filing. Observing her procedure from interview to finalisation, he assessed her as "very efficient" with "energy and initiative"—the "kind of girl you could play stickball on the street with." Following her own advice to Vivi Crespi to "become distinct," Jackie spent a significant amount of time figuring out how to transform the limits of a traditionally humdrum column into a refreshing bit of wisdom, wit, poignancy, and news. She would build a rhythm that reflected her odd tastes and make public the unexpected person who always lurked beneath the shell of glamour in a relatively short period of time.

"Like politics, there was no routine," she later remarked. There were no two days that were alike. "I enjoyed every second of it."

"If something interesting happened" in the news, Waldrop said, she would address it with a column question in real time. She'd rush back to the office, develop her photos, narrow down her final six picks from the 10 or so people she met, and do her daily struggle with the typewriter to transcribe her quotes. Jackie, like many creative types, worked until the wee hours of the morning to produce her best work—an unstructured schedule was her method of putting the column together. The column, which was published six days a week, averaged 144 individual interviews per month, amounting to roughly 2,600 people by the time she departed the post. "I wonder what happened to them," she told Waldrop, despite the fact that each day meant interviewing new people. I paused them for a moment—and they trusted me to respond.... They occasionally haunt me."

A significant portion of her earnings were spent on round-trip transit to see John in New York. While flying was faster, plane tickets every other weekend became prohibitively expensive for her. Aside from that, she still loved using the train. "She loved the efficiency of taking the plane, but it was never as relaxing for her as taking the train," a friend later remarked. In fact, one of her early editorials inquired, "Do you prefer to travel by train or plane?"

The Senator regional passenger train had been modified in early 1952 to offer "parlour service," which included a car with huge windows and plusher chairs where she could comfortably read. She made good use of her time: during Christmas, she had received an unexpected present of around a half dozen "precious books" from Father Leonard, to whom she then expressed her appreciation:

"You know what's wonderful about these books—I was really afraid that once I left college, I'd never learn again—just read best-sellers and maybe a couple of things like history I'd never learned and bit by bit forgot so much." And you keep me studying and introducing me to new realms."I could never do that by myself, no matter how badly I wanted to, because I didn't even know those books and authors existed—but it appears to me that you know everything and can pick and choose the most lovely things for me—Does it give you a sense of power to think you're moulding someone else's mind and taste? I hope it does, and no one has ever worked with a more willing piece of putty."

It appears that being in New York was less enjoyable than going there. Black Jack was delighted to see her more frequently, but he couldn't help but be upset that after dropping off her bags and hugging him, she had to change and dash out the door to supper with John Husted. While John's idea that they spend weekends with Unk and Mummy in Newport after their honeymoon was meant to be an inducement, Yusha claimed it made her "stomach drop," because she wished to travel to Europe.

John was likewise annoyed by her. Taking the train to save money meant spending less time together; they could only have Saturday and Sunday lunch before she had to leave. Failing to please her fiancé or her father became discouraging. It didn't take long for her to admit to a friend that meeting John involved "too much long distance."

Unbeknownst to him, she was looking forward to returning to Washington and the company of a very different John.

John B. White, eighteen years her senior, had an armful of tattoos and a love of history, reading, politics, and journalism. He referred to himself as a "frivolous scholar." He'd been a wartime combat correspondent for the Boston Herald Traveler and the Times-Herald. He'd recently moved to the State Department but kept in touch with his former Times-Herald colleagues; he first met Jackie when he dropped by to visit them. White and Jackie quickly bonded over their shared interests, and his basement flat, which had walls of books, became her haven in the winter and spring of 1952.

"I had the distinct impression she felt weary shuttling back and forth to New York," White remembered, noting that Husted was never mentioned. "After a while, she started spending her weekends around Washington, and she and I went out occasionally."

Jackie was overjoyed to discover White was a mythology scholar. When he took her to the city's mental institution, St. To interview its director, the trio engaged in a conversation on Hercules' psychology. She educated him as well through her love of Sappho's old lyric poetry. White was drawn to her, but she had a "undigested, renegade toughness at the very core of Jackie's personality... [she] intimidated a lot of people." He "certainly never tried anything" with her other from once holding her "big strong hand." He noticed she lacked "much, if any, sexual experience," but she wasn't "particularly afraid of it." Instead, they discussed ideas and projects. "We discussed her Inquiring Photographer column," he said. "She was brilliant at eliciting inquiries. She was inquisitive and skilled at winning people's trust; she got candid responses from her interview subjects. And she enjoyed discussing with her upper-class acquaintances what questions to pose to people in her column."

She sought inspiration for her column from a number of sources, including her personal hobbies and breaking wire-service news, in order to produce a column that was provocative enough to satisfy a varied readership. She'd take an office debate and see if it incited passersby in the same way. She admitted to modifying some comments to add drama and wit, but she realised she could only take so many liberties with remarks attributed to persons who were recognized by name; there is no evidence that anyone objected to how they were quoted. (There was one known instance of her pushing the envelope. She ascribed an answer to her stepsister Nini's inquiry about whether boarding school and college students were eager to return to campus, claiming that she preferred being at home and being free to "throw your clothes around the room in utter piggishness." She later said, "I never said that—Jackie answered it for herself."

Waldrop observed that she had both an unusual manner of thinking that led to startling questions and an instinct for asking what most readers would have been thinking. "Where does she come up with this stuff?" he wondered, concluding that her reading on a wide range of topics nourished her creativity. When the "B" volume of the newsroom encyclopaedia went missing, he discovered she'd kept it at her desk, studying the entry for "Bolivia." When he told her he'd teach her the so-called card game, she replied, "No, the country."

This unpredictability would aid in the growth and retention of her column's readership. Glen "Zeke" Hearing, Jackie's coworker, advised her to "dare to deviate" in her queries. She did this, for example, by seeking out the most unlikely demography for specific queries. Instead of asking ladies at luncheons, "What do you think of Dior's spring fashion line?" she waited on a street corner for truck drivers to stop at a red light and asked. At other instances, she poked fun at those with clearly defined characters, asking circus clowns, "Does your smiling face hide a broken heart?" as well as "Are you funny at home?" During the American Psychological Association meeting, she waited in a hotel lobby to confront recognized mental health specialists and ask, "How do you think you're maladjusted?"

Jackie aimed to do more than just entertain. She sought to excite and educate her readers, giving them the opportunity to better comprehend frustrating behaviour ("Why do you think people put off Christmas shopping until the last minute?" "Why do you think there are so many people who crack corny jokes in elevators?" "Do people welcome constructive criticism?") and grow in empathy ("What is the greatest need of people in the world today?" "What do people live for the most?" "What is the first thing you notice about people when you meet them?" Do you frequently have to modify your first impressions?"). She even managed to bring up a few existential issues ("Which came first, the chicken or the egg?"). "What is the best age?" The effort to bring out the best in strangers by pausing and encouraging them to think for themselves and own their brief moment of public attention was a small gesture, but it lifted the dignity and respect the individuality of otherwise overlooked citizens while engaging the minds of thousands of similar readers. While some columns might have been intended to encourage erudite pursuits ("If you were put in solitary confinement and could only take one book, which would it be?"), she never avoided esoteric questions on the presumption that a cleaning lady or clerk was uninterested in the topics ("In The Doctor's Dilemma, George Bernard Shaw asks if it's better to save the life of a great artist who is a scoundrel, or a commonplace, honest family man. "What are your thoughts?" "Do you think modern art reflects our times as much as Renaissance art did?") Because of the way she phrased the question, even someone unfamiliar with an author or historical period may make an informed response. She did not lecture the mostly working-class persons she interviewed; instead, she listened to them.

"You could make the column about anything you wanted," she recalled. So I'd go out and find a bunch of tough, salty characters and ask them about a prizefighter merely to record the way they spoke." Her best editing abilities were required for the process. She printed comments that often read like screenplay dialogue, with colourful euphemisms, slang, or aphorisms, in order to preserve the range of rhythm, dialect, and vocabulary she heard. She attempted to distil her responders' personality in fifty or so words; visually helped by a snapshot, each answer effectively shows a separate character.

In one post about southern charm, she interviewed Georgia Senator Richard Russell, Virginia Governor John Battle, and actress Tallulah Bankhead, whom she met at Alice Roosevelt Longworth's home. The actress, the daughter of a former Speaker of the House, did not disappoint: "My magnolia-scented southern charm has served me well, both professionally and privately." Many a boss has been melted, many a carpetbagger has been chilled, and many a swain has been perplexed. Its extravagant application has taken me from Huntsville, Alabama—that's [Senator] Sparkman's hometown—dash, you heard me—dash—to New York, London, Hollywood, and other places it would be impolite to discuss."

Jackie adored live performances, whether it was theatre, opera, or dance, and the column provided her an opportunity to ask the artists questions. She cornered actors in a National Theater production and asked them, "Why is there 'no business like show business'?" She went backstage to question the cast of Madama Butterfly at the Metropolitan Opera, "Do you think foreign language opera should be sung in English in this country?"

She subsequently noted that the finest interview subjects were youngsters because they "gave better answers than anyone," but she "most enjoyed" the interviews surrounding dance performances since they allowed her to spend "so much of the day with dancers at rehearsal." (She interviewed Ballets Russes dancers who let her sit in on rehearsals several times. "What do you think about while you're dancing?" she inquired.)

Jackie's column ideas were never suppressed, despite Waldrop's threat to fire her for asking pedestrians which local newspaper they preferred and printing comments that preferred the competition. Jackie was also astute enough to draw attention to the column by interviewing senators, cabinet members, Supreme Court justices, and members of the military services, as well as actor Jimmy Stewart when he came to town. Despite her ageless style, Jackie Bouvier had been interested in popular culture since she was a young adult. In boarding school and college, she wore her chestnut mane over one eye like movie stars Rita Hayworth and Veronica Lake, and she enjoyed swinging in a "wild jitterbug" to Glenn Miller and Benny Goodman big band music. She was bitten by the "Latin Craze" of the late 1940s, like millions of other Americans, as a high school student, enamoured with fashion, furnishings, and music inspired by South American civilizations. As a young reporter, she was equally aware of what was going on. She balanced her column's highbrow inquiries with those concerning pop culture, from the popularity of pinball machines to the marriage of the cartoon character Li'l Abner. When a flying saucer was spotted over Washington, she inquired as to what others thought it was. Marilyn Monroe, who had become a sex symbol by popularising the bikini five years earlier and was breaking through as an actress and singer, was a particular interest for her: "What would you talk about if you had a date with Marilyn Monroe?" "Do you think bikini bathing suits are immoral?" "Are women's clubs right in demanding that Marilyn Monroe be less suggestive?" "Do you truly believe diamonds are a girl's best friend?"

"You could make the column about anything you wanted," she recalled. So I'd go out and find a bunch of tough, salty characters and ask them about a prizefighter merely to record the way they spoke." Her best editing abilities were required for the process. She printed comments that often read like screenplay dialogue, with colourful euphemisms, slang, or aphorisms, in order to preserve the range of rhythm, dialect, and vocabulary she heard. She attempted to distil her responders' personality in fifty or so words; visually helped by a snapshot, each answer effectively shows a separate character. In one post about southern charm, she interviewed Georgia Senator Richard Russell, Virginia Governor John Battle, and actress Tallulah Bankhead, whom she met at Alice Roosevelt Longworth's home. The actress, the daughter of a former Speaker of the House, did not disappoint: "My magnolia-scented southern charm has served me well, both professionally and privately." Many a boss has been melted, many a carpetbagger has been chilled, and many a swain has been perplexed. Its extravagant application has taken me from Huntsville, Alabama—that's [Senator] Sparkman's hometown—dash, you heard me—dash—to New York, London, Hollywood, and other places it would be impolite to discuss."

Jackie adored live performances, whether it was theatre, opera, or dance, and the column provided her an opportunity to ask the artists questions. She cornered actors in a National Theater production and asked them, "Why is there 'no business like show business'?" She went backstage to question the cast of Madama Butterfly at the Metropolitan Opera, "Do you think foreign language opera should be sung in English in this country?"

She subsequently noted that the finest interview subjects were youngsters because they "gave better answers than anyone," but she "most enjoyed" the interviews surrounding dance performances since they allowed her to spend "so much of the day with dancers at rehearsal." (She interviewed Ballets Russes dancers who let her sit in on rehearsals several times. "What do you think about while you're dancing?" she inquired.)

Jackie's column ideas were never suppressed, despite Waldrop's threat to fire her for asking pedestrians which local newspaper they preferred and printing comments that preferred the competition. Jackie was also astute enough to draw attention to the column by interviewing senators, cabinet members, Supreme Court justices, and members of the military services, as well as actor Jimmy Stewart when he came to town. Despite her ageless style, Jackie Bouvier had been interested in popular culture since she was a young adult. In boarding school and college, she wore her chestnut mane over one eye like movie stars Rita Hayworth and Veronica Lake, and she enjoyed swinging in a "wild jitterbug" to Glenn Miller and Benny Goodman big band music. She was bitten by the "Latin Craze" of the late 1940s, like millions of other Americans, as a high school student, enamoured with fashion, furnishings, and music inspired by South American civilizations. As a young reporter, she was equally aware of what was going on. She balanced her column's highbrow inquiries with those concerning pop culture, from the popularity of pinball machines to the marriage of the cartoon character Li'l Abner. When a flying saucer was spotted over Washington, she inquired as to what others thought it was.

Marilyn Monroe, who had become a

CHAPTER 10

BYLINE

Jackie had a frantic social life while John Husted wasn't in town. Betty Beale described Jackie's attendance at a "Leap Year Dance," where she waited in line to dance with an air force general until four a.m., but the most memorable evening she enjoyed was with the young congressman from Massachusetts. In the final weeks of winter, she was invited to a dinner party at his brother Bobby's house in Georgetown by Jack Kennedy. It was their fourth meeting, and like with all of their prior encounters, they were joined by others. "Everything was done in groups," writer Page Huidekoper recounted of his time spent socialising with the youthful Kennedys and their friends. Lem Billings was among those she met as part of the group travelling to Bobby and Ethel Kennedy's dinner. In a period when homosexuality was often cause for rejection, neither Jack nor any of his family shunned Billings for being a "confirmed bachelor."

"I didn't know anything about Jackie until the first time I met her," Billings said. "I recall we were going to Bobby's for dinner... At the time, I was staying with Jack, and we drove out to Merrywood to pick up Jackie.... That was my first encounter with Jackie Bouvier. I recall him telling me she was a gorgeous young lady who was engaged to someone else.... When I met her, she was even wearing an engagement ring. I had met several of Jack's females throughout the years that I had known him, so this was simply another. It was intriguing that this girl was engaged.... To be honest, he didn't know her very well when I met her.... It wasn't anything exceptional at the time, except that she was an extraordinarily attractive lady, younger and prettier, I thought, than most of the others he dated."

Jackie told Molly Thayer about their first encounters: "Saw Jack occasionally that winter when he would come down to Washington." The congressman was in town on a rare occasion at the time. While waiting for Massachusetts Governor Paul Dever to determine whether to run for the U.S. Senate seat, Kennedy pressed ahead with his heavy speaking schedule in Massachusetts, convinced he could beat Lodge. When John White tried to talk him out of running, Jack reacted. "I never saw such passion in him," White exclaimed. John White admitted to being jealous of Jack Kennedy for having already published a book when they met a decade earlier, but was won over when the congressman "said that the most beautiful book he's ever read was Seven Pillars of Wisdom by T. E. Lawrence... the way he said it, it suddenly came out of nowhere and it was, it seemed to lift him out of being just... hard-driving to a thoughtful, somewhat compassionate man." White's great companion, Kennedy's late sister Kathleen, had introduced the two. Kathleen Kennedy and Inga Arvad (both having come to the paper on the recommendation of Arthur Krock, like Jackie) became friends in the end of 1941, shortly after White arrived at the Times-Herald, and Kathleen helped Inga write her column "Did You Happen to See?" Kathleen introduced Inga to Jack, a navy ensign working in Washington at the time. Despite the fact that she was married, Inga began a passionate affair with him. The foursome interacted in public to give the appearance that they were merely pals. Jack Kennedy had hardly dated a single woman seriously since his days at boarding school; they were his companions, occasionally sexual partners but never intellectual partners. In this scenario, Inga's abilities combined with her physical attractiveness. According to her biographer, "he had fallen in genuine love with her because she had listened to him as a way of understanding him, as a person, as a writer."

Arvad, a Columbia School of Journalism graduate, had previously worked as a freelance reporter in Berlin, infiltrating the Third Reich hierarchy and even interviewing Hitler, who saw her as a Nordic ideal and invited her to the 1936 Berlin Olympics as his guest. By the time she was working for the Times-Herald, the FBI was on her tail as a possible Nazi spy, reportedly after Frank Waldrop raised concerns about her to the FBI's director, J. Edgar Hoover. Hoover found out she was seeing Jack Kennedy just weeks before the United States went to war. Hoover wiretapped the couple, fearing she would try to gain critical information from the young navy ensign. Joe

Kennedy was notified, and he became concerned about how the affair may jeopardise Jack's career.

"One of ex-ambassador Kennedy's eligible sons is the target of a Washington gal columnist's affections," gossip columnist Walter Winchell wrote on January 12, 1942. Pa Kennedy does not approve." Inga's biographer believed that it was Joe Kennedy who tipped off Winchell in order to stop the relationship. As seen by Jack's later letters to Inga, their intellectual link and his love for her endured. Kennedy had found solace in having his sister's company after their divorce. The two were so similar that they were dubbed "the Kennedy twins." Kathleen departed for the United Kingdom to join the Red Cross in 1943. In May 1944, while Jack was resting in a Boston naval hospital from a severe back injury sustained when the PT-109 boat he commanded as a lieutenant was rammed by a Japanese ship, she married William Cavendish, the Marquess of Hartington. Cavendish perished in the battlefield four months later. Kathleen, a widow living in England, was killed in a plane disaster in May 1948.

With her column at the Times-Herald, in the same newsroom where Inga and Kathleen had worked, and her own association with John White, Jackie would inevitably evoke memories of the two women who had meant the most to Kennedy—a significant factor in Jack Kennedy's early perception of her. Jackie's work for the Times-Herald did not sit well with John Husted. His displeasure extended beyond the constraints it placed on their time together—he seemed to detest her enthusiasm for it. "You take it too seriously," he reportedly told her. He most emphatically did not. He said in a 1978 interview that he would "assist her with the Inquiring Camera Girl business, which was an insipid little job.... We'd go to supermarkets and ask people stupid questions." He said they joked together while she worked, but he knew she worked hard to create what he dismissed as "stupid questions." Husted may have been humiliated by having his fiancée's imagination on display six days a week. His hostility mocked the most important aspect of her life at the time, her writing.

Despite this, she was forced to "figure it out as soon as you can," as she had often urged Yusha during his vacillations regarding key decisions. In reality, newly unreported words show that Jackie found Husted insufferable even during their engagement; "a disaster," her lawyer pal Walter Sohier felt. "'You know what I like about him... He looks so good in tails,' she said." Jackie subsequently admitted to Molly Thayer that when she "realised that the most important thing in his life was making a dry martini," she knew she "didn't love him," and "broke the engagement." She drove him to the airport and returned the ring on March 16, 1952. Husted has always asserted that Janet discovered his lack of wealth and caused the split. He claimed Jackie wrote him a letter (which he never showed anyone) in which she advised him to disregard the "drivel" linking her to Jack: "[I]t doesn't mean a thing." According to what she claimed, Jackie Bouvier enjoyed being in love, but she did not love John. She later attempted to remove the incident from her tale, stating that "John Husted's name must never be used... I refuse to write his name down in history." Janet made sure everyone knew her daughter was back on the market by having Betty Beale explain in her March 23 Washington Evening Star column that she "decided they were rushing things a bit" and "called off their engagement."

Jackie stated in a letter to a British friend, Dan Samuel, that the decision had left her "rather confused," but added, "I know it was right to break it," adding that the pact "seemed very wrong." "I am ashamed that we both went into it so quickly and gaily, but I think the suffering it brought us both for a while afterwards was the best thing—we both needed something of a shock to make us grow up," she wrote to Father Leonard. I'm not sure whether John has—I haven't seen him and don't really want to, not out of spite—it's simply better if that all fades away and we forget we knew each other—but I know it's matured me and it's about time! The next time will be AWESOME, with a joyful ending."

Jackie had learned not to put her faith in wishful thinking. She certainly did not want to give up her privileged lifestyle, but judging by her efforts to launch larger and potentially more lucrative writing projects, she had not abandoned her belief that she could eventually earn a comfortable income, if not a large fortune, from a career she cared about. She improved her job prospects by focusing on the column, with the added benefit of leaving her "doing just fine" following the breakup. She went to the Irish Embassy to inquire about the significance of St. Patrick's Day for her March 17 column. It was "first and foremost a religious feast," according to Ambassador John Joseph Hearne, and it "brought into Ireland the civilization that was to mould Western Europe," according to one of his aides. Their brogues, on the other hand, "made me so homesick, he [a staff member] could hardly get me out of the place," according to Jackie. She emailed the column to Father Leonard with pride.

Her column nine days later was more routine, asking for opinions on musician Johnny Ray, but the day's conversation in Waldrop's office was more significant: despite the fact that she'd only been a columnist for eight weeks, he'd decided to give her another raise, to $45.50 per week (for an annual salary of $26,000). Eight months later, she had made the column her own, changing the title from "Inquiring Photographer" to "Inquiring Camera Girl." More important than the pay boost, the title, or the fact that she was the first woman to write the column, she was the first person to be granted a byline. Everyone in Washington saw the name "Jacqueline Bouvier" in print every day. She allowed herself a moment of quiet pride and a smile of self-deprecation in her message to Father Leonard: "I have my name on the column now. The 'Inquiring Photographer,' Jacqueline Bouvier, is staggering about the streets carrying her 50-pound camera, about which she knows nothing except how to press the shutter.

"It's really ridiculous," she conceded, "but it's a lot of fun."

CHAPTER 11

A SECOND DINNER

According to all accounts, their deeper bond took hold during the May 8, 1952, meeting at the Bartletts', in the same place where Jackie and Jack had met almost precisely a year before. Soon after the dinner, Jack Kennedy would tell anybody who would listen about how he "leaned across the asparagus and asked her for a date." Her rejoinder: "There was no asparagus that night." It was a little of stagy banter between two performers, Jack the romantic and Jackie the reality.

The evening—the fifth occasion, according to the record, on which they spent time together—would become the start of a romanticised public narrative, drawn from an arsenal of polished anecdotes to be used repeatedly in press accounts. Kennedy's father had earlier used this strategy. His recurrent public assertion that the death of his first son, Joe Jr., prompted him to draft Jack into politics was a "trite story," Jackie explained, to be used whenever "you get so tired of people asking for anecdotes."

After this supper, Jack began to mention Jackie to his family. Except for his mother, they'd all met her in Palm Beach five months before. Teddy remembers Jack making no mention of her attractiveness or social standing, but rather of "the column she wrote." "He got a real kick out of it, and he had a few clips that he clipped and showed to family members." It demonstrated her very distinct way of thinking about the world. "He said he read it all the time."

After the second Bartlett supper, the pair saw each other more frequently, albeit scheduling was difficult with Jack on the campaign trail. "My courting with Jack [was] while he was running for the Senate, so he was in Washington rarely," Jackie recalled of the time.

He'd phone me from Massachusetts and make plans for one evening. Dinner at the Bartletts' or Ethel and Bobby's was always fairly private. We either stayed there till he took me home or went to the movies." As she described it, his driving her home was their "only private time."

One frequently told story featured Jack's car breaking down in Merrywood's driveway in mid-June, after Unk and Mummy had returned from Europe but before they went for Newport. "He came tramping back to the house, and I gave him the keys to Uncle Hugh's car to get him home," Jackie recalled. Uncle Hugh was taken aback the next morning when he left for work to find his own automobile gone—and a broken down one with a Massachusetts licence blocking his driveway." The account implies that Jack had returned her to Merrywood far too late at night for them to inform her stepfather. However, Lem Billings stated that the couple's intimacy was limited to kissing in the congressman's parked car. By late spring, Kennedy had established a distinct classification for Jackie, exposing her to his most trusted and closed of groups, his family. "[N]ever once did this suitor propose they go off for a night or a weekend," as journalist Laura Berquist, who would become close to them both, observed. But that didn't mean he stopped seeing other women.

"Oh, there were several [girls he was dating]," his campaign staffer Jean Mannix recounted. "No one in particular." He was dating Ann McDermott at the time. This occurred during the [1952] campaign. She arrived in Washington with the intention of working for the government. Nothing piqued her interest, and she returned home in May. He saw her, but he was also seeing Jackie at the time. And they [McDermott and Kennedy] had a great friendship." Nonetheless, Mannix thought that by 1952, Jack Kennedy had decided "that he wanted to marry Jackie Bouvier." True or not, Jackie seemed sufficiently charmed by his attention to enjoy seeing him without regard for the outcome. However, Kennedy's primary distraction from Jackie was his campaign. He spent every summer weekend in Massachusetts, and then every day when Congress was in recess.

Social articles at the period indicate that they maintained their independence even when he was in Washington. For example, Jack went to the April 14 Cherry Blossom Ball without a date that year. She would go to Billy Martin's Tavern in Georgetown by herself, "with her camera," remembered John D. Lane, an administrative aide to Connecticut senator Brien McMahon.

On May 18, 1952, in the Worcester, Massachusetts, Hotel Sheraton, Kennedy hosted his first big campaign event, which became a trademark format: a "tea party," which depended on the participation of his sisters Eunice, Pat, and Jean, but especially his mother, Rose. An estimated four thousand women attended the Worcester tea party. Rose Kennedy first ascended a low platform lined with flowers and thanked the audience for their attendance; she then introduced Jack, who spoke for around thirty minutes, following which the family was greeted by an interminable line of women. They repeated the event in Holyoke, Springfield, Quincy, Fitchburg, Boston, and Brockton for the next six weeks, until the Fourth of July weekend, with Jack missing only the last one. The events resulted in large mailing lists of both party's female voters. Jackie was considering her own actions to develop her profession with the same tenacity. She'd only been the official "Inquiring Photographer" columnist for two months, but she was eager to break free from the column's constraints and begin producing complete feature pieces for the paper. She became resolved to interview Ted Williams, the legendary Boston Red Sox outfielder, when she learned from a coworker that he would be in town for an April 15 game against the host team, the Washington Nationals ("Nats"). The task was made more difficult since Williams might be nasty to the press. She had asked a male coworker, feigning ignorance, how she could effectively corner the ballplayer. He informed her it was impossible; the only place she could be certain of meeting him was in the locker room at Griffith Stadium—a place she knew she wouldn't be admitted to.

While April 15 came and went, Jackie remembered her colleague's warning that she wouldn't be allowed into the locker room as if it were a dare. On May 10, 1952, she got as far as the locker room door, but she was denied access in the days leading up to Washington's game versus Philadelphia. Some players thought having a lady near the locker room before a game was bad luck, but she caused enough of a disturbance by begging for interviews that the home team president, Clark Griffith, and manager Bucky Harris came out to speak with her. "Do you think the Nats will break out of their hitting slump?" She questioned first baseman Mickey Vernon, right fielder Jackie Jensen, shortstop Pete Runnels, and centre fielder Jim Busby. As the game began, Jackie returned to the office, where she found that fortune had been on her side that day, with the Nats breaking their losing streak with thirteen hits. Some players referred to her as a lucky mascot. "Jacqueline seems to have been exactly what our ball club needed," the Times-Herald boasted of its columnist to its sports fans. "A short time after she sweetly asked the Nats when they were going to start slugging again, the club exploded with thirteen hits and defeated the Athletics, 5-3."

It was a thrilling adventure for someone like Jackie Bouvier, who relished violating laws and propriety, to sneak unannounced into union conventions, walk along loading docks, or push her way backstage at theatres. As a reserved person, she found the most fundamental aspect of her work terrifying. She admitted that it was "sheer agony to stop perfect strangers from asking them questions."

The unusual image of the young woman with the large camera strolling the streets garnered stares even before she opened her mouth. Waldrop recalled Jackie devising a well-timed tactic of hiding her own face from her subject by raising the camera just as she finished asking the question and then snapping their picture, often momentarily blinding them with the flash, to deal with her anxiety about violating personal boundaries. She had to convince them to reveal their name, occupation, and sometimes their address after transcribing their response. Everette Severe vividly recalls her wearing sunglasses (tucked atop her head when she was indoors). Her camera, as well as her soon-to-be famous sunglasses, served as shields. Jackie was also refining her own, intriguing persona. Mac McCarrick, an NBC coworker, remembers Sever's conversational voice as evenly regulated; nevertheless, at times, she'd utilise a girlish, whispery tone, causing many to believe she was weak. This dichotomy of fragility and confidence concealed her genuine character, which was warm, earthy, informal, and prone to absurdity. But it was also a means for her to obtain power in social interactions and control over how others perceived her. Jackie was the director and producer of her life's scenes, rather than an actress who swapped roles in front of different audiences, as many cynically imagined.

Jackie's business and social lives flourished that spring, with cocktail parties and receptions, as well as increased absorption into Washington's most powerful circles. The invitation to the annual Gridiron Club Sunday reception was her biggest coup, demonstrating how rapidly she'd ascended in journalism circles. Political luminaries such as Republican Senator Bob Taft and his wife, Martha, former Commerce Secretary Averell Harriman, Nancy Kefauver (wife of influential Tennessee Democratic Senator Estes Kefauver), Alice Roosevelt Longworth, Chief Justice Fred Vinson, and Senator Margaret Chase Smith were in the reception line into the Statler Hilton's Congressional Room, where cocktails were served. The Inquiring Photographer was also mentioned in a social column in the Washington Evening Star, which saw "Arthur Krock talking to pretty, young Jacqueline Bouvier."

With Unk and Mummy gone, Jackie began holding her own lively Merrywood parties, proving her ascension. The prestigious positions of the largely "highly intelligent" male guests astounded John White as much as their being thirty to forty years her elder. He noted that she had "a great knack for inspiring [good conversation] and loved to see people enjoying themselves and being bright." White concluded that "Jackie took joy in engaging with and being close to guys who were doing important things, not necessarily as advisor so much as confidante... Her interest in people tended to be proportional to their prominence.... In her opinion of people, power and charisma seemed to trump all other attributes."

Dinah Bridge, a British friend of the Kennedys, was a houseguest of Robert and Ethel Kennedy in the dying days of June 1952. She remembers Jack and Jean joining them for breakfast one morning during her visit when "around the corner of the front door came this beautiful girl in riding clothes to pick up Jean to go riding." And not long after that, perhaps one or two nights later, she was invited to supper."

Days later, Jack invited Jackie to spend the Fourth of July weekend with his family in Hyannis Port, Massachusetts, at their summer house. Any planned weekend guests would have been vetted with Jack Kennedy's father first. Far more than Jackie Bouvier's haircut had changed in the six months since the Ambassador first met her in Palm Beach. Jackie's ambitions had grown increasingly grandiose. She'd won the byline for her column and then stamped it with her distinct imprint. Her ambition was to write front-page stories for the Times-Herald, but it was evident that this would not be enough. She desired even more. Even becoming a New Yorker writer, which she had seen as her ultimate goal, would not suffice. What she desired, though she had no idea how she would achieve it, was genuine power. Subtly, she had hinted at that vision through the questions she chose for her column and the replies she decided to print, which communicated to the public what was on her mind and what she considered cultural and political progress. Even in the capital of the world's most powerful nation, a popular local daily column barely created a global platform. Jackie Bouvier aspired to greater things.

Joe Kennedy probably certainly knew where Jacqueline was going before she landed at Hyannis Port. As his daughter, Kathleen, had revealed to John White a decade before, the Ambassador casually but thoroughly scrutinised anybody who became close to one of his children, learning not just their place in the world but also their strengths and weaknesses. Having already given each of his children a million dollars (about $17 million in today's currencies) so they could "tell me to go to hell," he was on the lookout for con artists, swindlers, and fraudsters who would try to take advantage of them. "My father was impressed by her," Eunice Kennedy recalled, "which impressed me." It didn't matter to him that Jackie wasn't the heiress her demeanour represented, nor was she as French as her surname, Sorbonne degree, and language skill led people to believe (she was only one-eighth French). What undoubtedly wowed the Ambassador even more than her elegant exterior was his sense that she was secretly aiming for something bigger. "It's not what you are that counts," he famously said, "but what people think you are."

PART 6

"Maybe I'm just dazzled and picture myself in a glittering world of crowned heads and Men of Destiny… very glamorous from the outside—but if you're in it—and you're lonely—it could be Hell."

—JACKIE, TO HER FRIEND FATHER JOSEPH LEONARD

CHAPTER 12

HYANNIS PORT

Two days before Jackie went to Cape Cod to spend the Fourth of July with the Kennedy family, Metro-Goldwyn-Mayer released the results of a survey of 300 Washington news correspondents: Jack was named the "Handsomest" congressman. Months before, a nationally syndicated story hinted at his contentment on the field. "Attractive as any current Hollywood movie star," Associated Press reporter Jane Eads wrote. "He entertains a lot and gets around, but he's so far resisted the march to the altar."

That weekend, Jackie's priority was Joe, not Jack. "I had already met Jack's father when I'd gone for a weekend at the Palm Beach house [in December 1951]," she recalled. "He was the same—so warm and friendly. He was my hero." The merciless titan was not prone to gratuitous generosity unless he felt an individual worthy of his energy and, even better, that they might offer some type of quid pro quo to support his bigger aims. He saw right once that she possessed all of the attributes to be a perfect spouse for Jack, and so was well worth his time. Joe's stories of FDR and his advisers Harry Hopkins, Cordell Hull, and Harold Ickes, as well as Winston Churchill, captivated Jackie. "They would talk about everything," Jack and Jackie's friend Bill Walton, who knew them individually, said of Joe and Jackie. She entirely relied on him, trusted him, and grew to adore him."

It was a two-way road. "Joe soon became Jackie's most ardent supporter," Lem Billings explained. "He admired her for her individuality." She was not scared of him. She taunted him, cajoled him, spoke back to him.... She was conquering his son by conquering him."

One observer described their symbiotic relationship as a "sense of fun that almost excluded the rest of the family." Instead of the classic narrative that they thought her a little too precious, jealousy of this newcomer's immediate bond with the Ambassador may have been an unnoticed component in the icy attitude Jack's sisters and his sister-in-law, Ethel, demonstrated toward her. There was no conflict, but there was apparent tension at times.

"Meals were much fun, never dull, and very noisy," Dinah Bridge recalled of Kennedy dinners, adding, "so many laughs the whole time." "There was a tremendous amount of exciting discussion about everything that was going on," Chuck Spalding added, the Ambassador dominating.[T]here was no doubt about his point of view. As you could expect, he said it rather forcefully. They were not scared to differ, but they were not disobedient."

"While there was tremendous respect for the head of the family, always at dinner or in any company—if he had anything to say, and they would wait for him to say it—they all felt perfectly free to express, in very respectful terms, complete differences of opinion with their father," Arthur Krock observed. He'd claim they didn't have any sense or were 'idiots,' and... 'Jack is stating everything I don't believe in.' But it didn't appear to affect him."

Initially, Jackie may have misjudged how strong the rule of challenging the Ambassador was, resulting in an episode that, ironically, would endear her to him even more. Joe Kennedy kept clocks in each bedroom so that there was never an excuse for being late for meals, which irritated him much. Joe was not pleased when Jackie arrived fifteen minutes after lunch had begun. "So," Spalding remembered, "he started to give her the needle, but she immediately returned it." 'You ought to create a series of grandfather stories for children, like, The Duck with Moxie, and The Donkey Who Couldn't Fight His Way Out of a Telephone Booth,' she advised him. The room fell silent almost immediately. Nobody in his family dared to speak to him with such sarcasm. Then, all of a sudden, he burst out laughing, releasing the tension and winning over. Other distinctions existed between the Kennedy home and those Jackie knew. The Bouvier and Auchincloss summer weekend festivities were formal in both attire and cuisine. Rose Kennedy always offered Boston baked beans and brown bread on Saturday nights, along with grilled steaks, hamburgers, and hot dogs, with the remaining beans warmed up for Sunday breakfast.

After supper, they played games including Telephone, Charades, Sardines (a variation on Hide-and-Seek), and Ambassador (in which one member of a team's imagined renowned identity must be guessed by the other team). "It's incredible how good Jackie was at these games," Billings said of his former teammate. "Jackie's background of constant reading and her quickness of thought in these areas made her much better than [Jack]," he went on to say. "It always irritated him because she was obviously better at these things than he was, and it just drove him insane."

That weekend, she also went sailing with Jack and his siblings, which was probably their favourite activity. She discovered the waters off Cape Cod for the first time, which were colder than East Hampton and had a less rugged coastline than Newport.

"It was the first time I'd seen all of Jack's family together.... It was the first time I'd seen all of Jack's family together.... What can I say about those people? They tasted like carbonated water.... They'd be discussing so many topics with such zeal. Otherwise, they'd be playing games. Everyone would be talking about something over dinner or in the living room. It was quite stimulating for them since they were so interested in life. And so gay, kind, open, and accepting of outsiders. They were fantastic, in my opinion."

During the weekend, Jackie met Rose, who was equally interested in European history and was working on improving her French and German. Mrs. Kennedy attributed her discipline to severe, ancient Catholic dietary restrictions (Friday abstinence from meat and fasting before receiving Holy Communion). She expected the same of her children, pushing them to be "morally, mentally, and physically perfect as possible," and admitting to using rulers and coat hangers on them when they were younger. Rose thought Jack was "very interested in people and social issues." He was always reading.... He was quite attractive. "A fantastic athlete." She also singled him out for always being late for family supper, "every day." It wasn't simply "poor discipline," she explained, but also "deliberate."

Jackie may have thought Rose to be similar to Mummy in certain ways. Whereas Janet scoffed at her daughter's "wild imagination," Rose sneered that Jack "did things his own way, and somehow just didn't fit any pattern[, which] distressed me." Jackie was also prone to binge reading and arriving late for family gatherings, breaking maternal expectations. Rose, like Mummy, might get obsessed with her son's looks, noting that he was "careless about his clothes."

Jackie noticed in the family relationships that Jack had "such a strong personality—like his father, who has so overpowered Mrs. Kennedy that he doesn't even speak to her when she's around, and her only solace now is her religion." I don't think Jack's mother is particularly bright—she'd rather say a rosary than read a book.Polly Fitzgerald, a relative of Jack's mother, said he "had a shyness about him." "He liked people, but putting himself in the spotlight wasn't easy for him." So did his visitor. Jackie looked around the Kennedy home at the childhood books, particularly King Arthur and the Knights of the Round Table, that Jack had relied on as a boy when he was isolated due to a series of early illnesses; for Jackie, it had been her parents' divorce and acrimony that had inspired her to seek solace in literature. Their similar desire for in-depth reading was noteworthy. Unlike Jackie, who had read the complete works of Shakespeare and Dumas, Jack had devoured Winston Churchill's five volumes on World War II, as well as his father's multivolume The World's Great Orations, which covered every period from the ancient Greek philosophers onward, and she recalled, "[H]e read that set through from beginning to end."

Teddy, Jack's youngest sibling, and she hit it up right away. Their friendship was easy, as they freely discussed issues ranging from colonial Boston through the Civil War. He related how Jack had "bragged" about Jackie before she joined them for the holiday. Whatever Jack said Jackie about Joe Jr. left her thinking of him as "a bully for an older brother." The worst indictment, in her opinion, was the single most important characteristic she believed a man should have. "I have a feeling, based on what I think of Joe [Jr.] and everything, that he would have been so unimaginative in comparison to Jack," she acknowledged honestly. "I don't think he had the same kind of imagination as Jack."

However, the entire family was unified and engrossed in one huge compelling crusade: getting their beloved Jack elected to the unified States Senate. The campaign team was led by Dave Powers and political operatives Larry O'Brien and Kenny O'Donnell, but the Ambassador insisted on acting as king, causing the others to avoid him during meetings. And it wasn't just in private that the Ambassador was difficult. Allegations of antisemitism made public threatened Jack's support among Jewish voters. He also held political ideas that were diametrically opposed to those of his son. In January, he wrote an editorial for Waldrop urging Democrats to back Republican senator Robert Taft if he won his party's presidential nomination that year, in order to weed out the "socialist-labour czars who have gained control of [the Democratic party]." He had also previously stated, contrary to his son, that the US should withdraw from Korea. When asked about his father's isolationism, Jack stated unequivocally that his father had the right to his views, but that he had established his own.

By the summer, Bobby Kennedy had taken over as campaign manager, posting a wall-sized map of every city and town where the candidate had spoken in Jack's Boston apartment (which served as headquarters at the time). When complaints about Jack's absenteeism in Congress began emerging in the Springfield Union, the Haverhill Gazette, and other Massachusetts newspapers in early June, he cancelled his speeches and sent Bobby on the campaign tour in his place.

Bobby was in charge of every action that carried his brother's campaign to victory. Even the anecdotal notion that his wife had christened Miss Bouvier "the Deb" may have been founded in a bigger, unstated strategy devised to capitalise on Jack's solitary marital status. Any public indication that he was dating a lady important enough to be considered a future spouse, the argument ran, would dampen the enthusiasm of thousands of female voters who had crushes on him, and would even prevent them from voting.

The Republican National Convention opened in Chicago on Jackie's first day back at work in Washington after her weekend on Cape Cod. By the end of the week, its delegates had nominated General Dwight D. Eisenhower for president and California Senator Richard Nixon for vice president. Two weeks later, Democrats nominated Illinois governor Adlai Stevenson for president and Alabama U.S. Senator John Sparkman for vice president at the same arena.

Jackie began to ask column questions about the presidential race almost immediately, ranging from "What do you think of General Eisenhower winning the nomination on the first ballot?" and "What do you think of Governor Stevenson's nomination?" to "With which Presidential candidate would you rather be marooned on a desert island?" and "How should elderly health care be provided?" and many more.

While Jackie's sudden obsession with political topics for the column appeared compulsive, with one inquiry after another, it was all new to her. The Bouviers, Lees, and Auchinclosses were staunch Republicans; when she was misbehaving, the two names used to frighten her into good behaviour were Bruno Hauptmann, the kidnapper of the Lindbergh infant, and President Roosevelt. Her young political interest was limited to collecting presidential campaign buttons backing Wendell Willkie's Republican candidacy in 1940 and General MacArthur's in 1944. However, by 1952, she looked to have evolved into a true independent, judging politicians on their ideas; later, her friend Arthur Schlesinger discovered that Stevenson was "the first political voice to whom she listened."

She couldn't help but notice another one.

CHAPTER 13

SUMMER IN THE CITY

When Jackie returned to work following the holiday weekend, Waldrop had left for the summer, and Sidney Epstein had taken over as her immediate employer. A drowsiness set in. Washington's infamous mugginess worsened, posing a productivity issue. Despite the fact that the newsroom was on the first floor and had wide windows that could be opened, there was no cross breeze other than what was provided by large floor fans. Working inside was uncomfortable without the relatively recent occurrence of industrial air conditioning. It was even terrible hitting her on the pavement.

"How do you keep cool?" she inquired that summer "in various hot spots" throughout the city. Bobby Donaldson, a short-order cook, said watermelon; little Mark Miller said ice cream (and when his mother didn't give him money, "I ask my dad"); model Betty Jean Cullen drank iced tea; student Susan Shephard went swimming; and fair-skinned housewife Carey Brent wore a large, protective hat ("You can remove freckles with buttermilk, you know"). Jackie's favourite response came from bookseller Thomas Fitzgerald: "Are you being facetious? You're talking to the Supreme Sufferer. I sweat, darling lady, and I don't keep cool. "I sweat and think of Omar Khayyam's immortal lines: 'Oh paradise, what I wouldn't give for a piece of ice.'"

The work might become "something of a grind" for Jackie Bouvier, according to Times-Herald society reporter Angela Gingras, but she "managed to maintain a sense of humour about it." She remembered stumbling into her on the scorching streets, "wandering around with her camera slung over her shoulder, looking for interesting people to photograph and interview.""She grinned and asked me how business was going—as one lady walking the Washington equivalent of the Boulevard des Italiens to another," Jackie explained. Miss Bouvier was alluding to the Parisian street prostitutes. To make matters worse, with so many people she knew fleeing the inferno for colder climes, her social life came to a halt. Jackie had a huge edge that summer because Merrywood had a pool. She refused Jack Kassowitz and other reporters' requests to leave the office and go to "your pool this afternoon," but she let John Husted's three Washington relatives use it. Jackie was back at work once she got home, and not just on her column. Jackie had heard whispers about the Octagon House, an obscure brick structure with an unusual design on the corner of New York Avenue and 18th Street, in June. It was one of the city's oldest structures, built in 1798 and having survived the city's destruction during the War of 1812, and was rumoured to be haunted. She'd become so fascinated by the weird tales surrounding the location that she'd decided to develop a TV script for a program about the possibly haunted house. Jackie began composing the voice-over narration about the initial owner, the architect, the interior, the history of its use over the centuries, incidents that had occurred there, and five individual ghost stories after organising her script into six portions with an overview. She transmitted acutely precise visual sequences, as she had done in her Vogue essays, this time accompanied by suitably creepy narration. The script included ghost stories about the first mistress of the house hearing strange bell-ringing, her daughter committing suicide over an ill-fated romance with a British officer, her niece tripping over a black cat and falling down the sweeping staircase to her death, and the murder of an enslaved woman.

Jackie then sought advice on how to have her script produced. Despite Unk's extensive network, she had no contacts in the film or television industries, and as friendly as she was with the Ambassador, she didn't feel comfortable asking for his assistance. Although she was not a formal member of the National Press Club, many of her coworkers were, and she frequently went there after work for cocktails with others in journalism and similar businesses. She first met utilities lobbyist Stephen M. Walter, president of his own public relations firm, at the club. He was a native Kansan and former reporter who was familiar with Jackie's column. He was 62 years old. Despite his conventional appearance as a farm state Republican, Walter moonlighted as an inventor and volunteered to serve as a producer for her project, seeking broadcast outlets and finance. Black Jack and his daughters have avoided spending time together in East Hampton for the previous three summers. He might have skipped going to avoid his sister Edith, who had continued to spend without a budget, charging things directly to her trust, which Jack was forced to pay from her principal. To avoid depleting the Beale trust, he had begun to spend his own money to cover some of her costs. Already coping with extreme stress as a result of his feud with Edith over the family inheritance, he was struck by such crippling pneumonia in August that he said he nearly "kicked the bucket." He intended to sell his Stock Exchange seat after the market value increased "because my health will not allow me to continue in this business any longer." He had been a broker for 33 years at the time, but employment had "taken its toll on my health over the last three years."

While Jackie was juggling her column and her documentary script, her sister Lee was enjoying Newport's bright days and chilly evenings. Jackie came up for a few days at the end of August, persuaded by Mummy. The sisters threw a cocktail party and modelled for Newport Hospital in a fundraising drive.

Jackie joined Mummy and Unk after Labor Day for the seventh World Bank Conference in Mexico City, which began on September 5, 1952—her first visit to that country. The meeting lasted a full week and was held at the Del Prado Hotel. Jackie was yearning for an adventure after having written a week's worth of pieces ahead of time and having visited all of the city's museums. Mummy erupted in rage when she learned of Jackie's plan to "roam wild" and explore the coastal city of Acapulco. Jackie went despite their disagreement. Jackie noted, "[I] loved Acapulco"; it would become one of her favourite vacations. While visiting the area, she was drawn to a pink stucco home with staggered green slate that rose above the aqua water. The "charming house" was the one "I'd always thought I'd like to spend my honeymoon in." Marriage was obviously on her thoughts once more. While Mummy returned to Newport to serve as the arrangements chairman for a mid-September opera talk, Lee's competitiveness remained. Jackie had only been at Vogue for a week, but after Labor Day, Lee landed a coveted job as an assistant to the magazine's famed editor, Diana Vreeland, whose son Freaky was a friend of Jackie's. Yusha greeted Jackie as she arrived home. He had just finished his second tour of duty with the Marines and was in town to take a class at the School of Advanced International Studies, a subsidiary of Johns Hopkins University situated in Washington, to prepare for his studies at the American University of Beirut the following school year. Yusha revitalised Jackie's social life near the conclusion of the summer. They'd invite two "interesting" pals chosen for intriguing conversation to join them for supper and a swim after his class and her day at the paper. "After we finished," he said, "we'd talk about the questions she'd asked during the day, and who she'd seen who she found particularly enlightening." He was disturbed by her lowering mood about her perceived lack of romantic desirability once they were alone. He later reflected on this period, saying, "She never understood her own charm or beauty." She had never considered herself to be attractive. She wasn't sure if anyone would be interested in her."

When one considers the frequency of her columns devoted to self-reflection and mental health, Jackie's admittance of spiralling melancholy and harsh self-analysis seems less shocking. ("What kind of compliment would you most like to receive?" "What are the best and worst things about yourself?" "When were you the most scared?" "What have you learned from your experience?" "What is your cure for the blues?" "Do you believe there is a Dr. Jekyll and Mr. Hyde in all of us?" "Of all the heinous things you've done, which one are you most ashamed of?")

Her mood was directly related to the fact that, by the time she returned from Mexico, she was becoming increasingly insecure about the ambiguous nature of her connection with Jack Kennedy. They hadn't seen each other in over two months. Others were picking up on it. A coworker asked for her own response while she was carefully typing her question of the day, "Who is the most fascinating man in the world to you?" "He's already left town to run for something or other," she hedged, adding cryptically. And you'd laugh if I told you. And, on top of that, he couldn't be less interested in me."

The best she could describe the connection was "spasmodic." It wasn't a case of envy. There were ladies he might take to dinner and others he might have slept with, but no women he was dating seriously at the moment. After up to fifteen-hour days of speeches and public appearances, he could be found alone in Schrafft's on Boylston Street, sipping a double-chocolate Coke or eating flounder at the Union Oyster House. Jack Kennedy won his party's nomination for the Senate seat two days after Jackie returned from Mexico, and there was a brief respite in his campaign schedule. She remembered him calling her "from some oyster bar up there, with a great clinking of coins, to ask me out to the movies the following Wednesday." She invited him to join her and Yusha for an evening at Merrywood while he was in town. Before Jack Kennedy came, Jackie admonished Yusha, saying, "I don't want you to argue with him because you're a conservative and he's a liberal." You attended Yale. He attended Harvard. You visited Groton. He attended Choate. You used to be a marine. He served in the navy. But... you're both interested in foreign policy." While she cooked hamburgers on the grill, she urged him to create the lime daiquiris that she and Jack both enjoyed. "I liked him very much," Yusha wrote of Jack. And we never argued... he was always asking questions and was a fantastic listener... [and] a really gracious individual.... Jackie sought chivalry, grace, charm, and fearlessness in men, and he possessed all four." Yusha wrote in his notebook on Tuesday, September 23, that Kennedy returned the next night: "Jack cooked our supper and drove me to the train." I met John White on the way." But, with her stepbrother's departure to Beirut shortly after, Jackie was once again alone in her thoughts. Jack Kennedy went just as swiftly as he had returned, eager to get back to campaigning in Massachusetts. Jackie began to wonder if their lifestyles were too dissimilar. According to Father Leonard, Jack's presence in her life provided her with "an amazing insight on politicians—they really are a breed apart."

Perhaps it wasn't so much his way into politics as it was the zeal with which he pursued his ambitions that gave her pause. She saw Jack as "consumed by ambition 'like Macbeth.'" But she, too, had a great determination—once she set her sights on something, she pursued it with zeal: admittance into the Sorbonne, an extended stay in Europe, winning the Vogue contest, and landing her columnist post.

She disclosed everything to Father Leonard in one of the most revealing letters of her early life. Distance may have provided her with the opportunity to "write all this down and get it off [my] chest—because I never really do talk about it with anyone." She wrote down what she had not yet felt comfortable discussing with anybody else, even Yusha, after reflecting on her time with the Kennedys. "Maybe it will end very happily—or maybe, since he's this [35 years] old and set in his ways and cares so desperately about his career, he just won't want to give up that much time to extracurricular things like marrying," she thought with a certainty and seriousness she hadn't had before. If he ever asks me to marry him, it will be for very practical reasons—his career is his driving force.... Perhaps I'm merely enchanted and imagine myself in a sparkling realm of crowned heads and Men of Destiny—rather than just a lonely little housewife.... That world may appear to be very glamorous from the outside, but if you're in it and lonely, it may be Hell."

The five most telling words in her confession to Father Leonard were "I think I'm in love."

"I worked on the paper [Times-Herald] all fall," Jackie said of her regular days after Labor Day in 1952. "It was election season, and I didn't see much of Jack." When she did see him, her perception of him would change dramatically.

She was rewriting her documentary script alongside the column. She had hinted to Waldrop last spring that the rising influence of television as a medium for entertainment might well hold true for news as well. By autumn, she was fully committed to that goal. Everybody was. By the end of 1952, almost twenty million American households owned a television set, a 33 percent increase from the previous year, when Jackie began working at the newspaper. American advertisers spent 38.8 percent more money on television advertising over the same one-year period, totaling $288 million.

Her script was fifteen pages long, indicating that she purposefully crafted her Octagon House documentary for television, with the typical rate being one page per minute of broadcast to be slotted into a half hour; half of the airtime was allowed for advertising. Stephen Walter "only made suggestions" to the script, according to his wife, Martha. He then addressed several of his public relations clients and found one who was interested in funding her initiative; in the meantime, Jackie created her own relationship with the local CBS Television affiliate, WTOP, as a prospective broadcast venue. (She wasn't crazy to ask Waldrop if the Times-Herald had a TV station; the Washington Post had bought a stake in the station two years before.)

WTOP was noted for its high-quality and early colour programming transmission. CBS Films was founded that year as a syndication service capable of distributing local affiliate programming to hundreds of additional stations across the country. She sent her revision to Stephen Walter, joking that if a TV contract didn't work out, she was willing to reimagine it as a two-hour dramatic feature-film script:

"This is it. I have 50 million more facts, but putting them all in would be too much. I attempted to spice it up with romantic suicides and lovers' encounters, but I don't think I did it well. Don't you think we could load it on and sell it to Louis B. Mayer as a co-starrer for Errol Flynn and Marilyn Monroe if CBS doesn't want it?"

Jackie's enthusiasm for television was mirrored by Jack's interest in it. He'd already made two national television appearances, on NBC's

Meet the Press on December 2, 1951, and on CBS's Longines Chronoscope on March 12, 1952. Recognizing television's potential to reach every home in the state, Jack thought up Coffee with the Kennedys, a late-morning television show aimed at housewives. Thousands of cards were issued to those attending the teas, inviting them to host "coffee hours" at home and ask their friends to come watch. Perhaps not coincidentally, Jackie asked in her column, "If both were on TV at the same time, which would you watch, the convention or the World Series?" and "Do you think that televising the convention will lead to more intelligent voting?"

On October 15, Kennedy arrived at the WNAC-TV studio in Boston with his mother and sisters. Eunice was dressed in a poodle skirt with his name written across it. "The Yankee Network" showed Rose, Jean, and Pat sitting in front of a big silver coffee set on a low coffee table, with the mother pouring some into china cups for her daughters. Jack and Eunice sat across the room at a white-clothed table, taking live phone calls from viewers. Though Black Jack had instilled in Jackie the conviction that "[p]politics is no place for women," Jackie's essays that summer and fall demonstrated that she was beginning to challenge that tenet: "Should women become more active in politics?" "How has the League of Women Voters affected your community?" "Would you support a woman running for President of the United States?" "Should a candidate's wife campaign in tandem with her husband?" All of the Kennedy women Jackie had grown to know were certainly in the press, doing their part for Jack. In the morning, Ethel Kennedy was photographed in a hospital bed with her newborn son, Joseph, before returning to campaign later that day, while Jean Kennedy was shown bringing presidential daughter Margaret Truman to Massachusetts. Rose advertised in the media that she would fly directly from Paris to discuss the fashion trends she saw there with the women of Massachusetts, which increased attendance at a September tea. Jackie spent the last weekend of October in Newport, where Mummy and Unk were preparing to relocate the family to Merrywood for the winter. It's unclear whether she called Jack to let him know she'd be close or he made the call, but the upshot was an offer to visit him on the campaign trail. The encounter would demonstrate to Jackie how important female voters were to his Senate campaign approach. Jackie arrived in Boston on Sunday, October 26. The day's events were highlighted by presidential contender Adlai Stevenson, but Jack was his co-star. They went from Boston to Quincy in an open automobile, where the candidates spoke on a platform outside the local high school. They then went to Cambridge for a Unitarian church service before returning to Boston for lunch and stopping in Taunton and New Bedford for an Israel-bond demonstration. Jackie joined Jack's sisters to Fall River for the campaign's most recognized and exuberant tea party, which began at 2:45 p.m. Four thousand people packed the massive armoury. According to the Boston Globe, few people ever "reached the tea and cookies."

The motorcade returned to downtown Boston as twilight fell, the setting sun leaving behind a biting New England chill. Hundreds of people lined the streets, cheering Stevenson and Kennedy on. The Kennedys and their entourage, together with Governor Dever, who had met Vice President Alben Barkley at the airport, walked through confetti to a big night rally at Mechanics Hall in Boston. Jean and Pat were granted honorary seats at the front of the podium and introduced by Boston's mayor. Humphrey Bogart and Lauren Bacall warmed up the audience. Thousands of supporters chanting "Adlai!" spilled out into Huntington Avenue from the crammed hall to hear Stevenson's speech, which was relayed over the loudspeaker. It was a three-ring circus like Jackie had never seen before. Following that, she and the sisters retired to Jack's two-bedroom apartment on the third story of 122 Bowdoin Street, across the street from the state capitol building's gold dome. Rose had repurposed several of her chintz chairs and curtains, as well as a floor lamp, a federal-style bureau, a bookcase, and a desk. Jack was rarely there alone; his siblings were frequently in and out, and while their parents were in town, they stayed in a suite at the Parker House hotel. Although Jack maintained an official congressional office on Kilby Street, the early strategy sessions for his campaigns had always started at his apartment since 1948. Jean's living room was packed with card tables where mailing lists of donors and supporters were being compiled. Members of his Washington staff would occasionally work from the apartment. Jackie believed the place was packed, and later told

Eunice that she thought it symbolised how his public role dominated his private life.

According to the October 3 Congressional Quarterly News Feature, the Kennedy campaign was a "frank play" for the women of Massachusetts, who were believed to account for 52 percent of the state's overall electorate. As campaign staffer Edward Berube phrased it uncomfortably, he remembered Jack suggesting that "the woman was the one who was going to put him in." At one of the tea parties, Jack stated that he hoped he was "impressing the feminine electorate." He and his team were still concerned that if word came out that he had a particular someone in his life, much alone the former Deb of the Year, it would significantly limit his attractiveness to female voters. According to John Droney, a campaign volunteer, "every unmarried woman had that hope and dream that lightning would strike."

Kennedy's tactics paid off on election night. With a record 90.94 percent of eligible voters in the state voting, and over 90 percent of women voters in major cities voting, he won by a 1.5 percent edge, just 70,737 votes more than Lodge. It is expected that roughly twice as many women attended the tea. Given Eisenhower's victory over Stevenson, the slim victory was all the more astonishing.

Meanwhile, Jackie and her large camera made their way into the Republican election night headquarters at Washington's Statler Hilton. "How do you feel now?" She addressed the party faithful (including Stevenson's Republican cousin Ashton Embry), who had brought an end to the Democratic Party's two-decade reign on the presidency. In Jackie's mind, the overnight shift in power was as visceral as a coup, and she managed to interview the outgoing Democratic attorney general, the U.S. Treasury secretary, the Secretary of the Senate, a presidential assistant, and Ambassador Perle Mesta for her column about what they planned to do on their first day out of power. She also questioned government servants about their feelings about working with Republicans, as well as members of the general public about who they wished to see nominated to Eisenhower's cabinet. Whether or not it was due to Jack's influence, her column consistently focused on contemporary political issues. She brought up Eisenhower's contentious nomination of Clare Boothe Luce as ambassador to Italy, but she also campaigned for more women to be chosen to executive branch positions. In response to a press inquiry, shortly after Jack endorsed President-elect "Ike" Eisenhower's trip to Korea, Jackie posed Jack's follow-up question (without crediting him): she asked people if they thought Ike should meet with General MacArthur before going, and the majority of her respondents were against it. Her own prospects were improving. An executive at the local CBS network read her Octagon House documentary script and "bought it," according to Stephen Walter's wife Martha. The network intended to have it made for one of the station's half-hour shows. Jackie also supposedly managed to get a little piece published in Time magazine around this time, though it didn't bear her byline and the subject remains unknown, with the only known mention to it being in a letter from Yusha, "to congratulate you on the clipping in Time." "[I] expect you will be receiving a much more interesting and enviable position in the paper in the very near future," he said as an afterthought, describing her exact objectives at that stage in her career. You more than deserve it."

Jackie Bouvier knew early on at the Times-Herald that no matter how unique or fascinating her columns were, she needed a boost to further her writing career. Her Nats column drew greater attention to her, but it was fleeting. She needed a story that would put her on the front page. One local beat had the most potential for national, if not international, coverage. So Jackie began to linger outside the nation's most famous residence.

"Jackie was especially fascinated with everything about the White House," Mini Rhea recounted. "She was always asking White House reporters, both male and female, about their jobs and telling them how lucky they were to work there." "Everything about the White House piqued her interest." She stopped guests, members of the press, and workers as they exited 1600 Pennsylvania Avenue in search of something she could turn into a bigger story. Her queries were frequently general in nature, such as "What are your memories of Presidents?" "Would you like your son to grow up and become President?" "Which First Lady would you have liked to have been?"—Some were sharper and more politically direct, referencing Truman's directive to set aside tidewater areas as navy reserves and asking, "Should these oil reserves be held for national defence?"

During the campaign, much attention had been paid to Ike's running partner, Richard Nixon, and Jackie knew readers were eager to discover more about the incoming vice president. (Earlier in the summer, she had asked his four-year-old daughter, Julie, "Do you play with Democrats?" causing her to question, "What's a Democrat?")

Three days after the election, as interest in Richard Nixon grew, Jackie located the location of his private residence and went there, loitering outside the house long enough to question several neighbours, "What do you think of Nixon now?" They were a housewife with a newborn on whom Nixon's children dotted; another whose dog played with Nixon's dog; the daughter of a Truman undersecretary with a direct view of his home; a five-year-old playmate of his eldest child, Tricia; and then Tricia Nixon herself, at the age of six. The child's reaction was direct: "He's always gone." Why can't he stay at home if he's famous? Have you seen this image? That's a welcome home gift I created for Daddy. Julie did one as well, but she doesn't colour as well as I do. My entire class was voting for Eisenhower, but I informed them I was just voting for Daddy.``

After months of depressing national election news, Jackie's discussion with Tricia Nixon provided a humanising break, and the story was syndicated, appearing in newspapers across the country. She'd made her own opportunity after a year of venting to Waldrop about how he wasn't assigning her the feature articles she claimed she was capable of producing. Jackie Bouvier received her first national exposure as a reporter. She had just gone where she was not supposed to, just as she had done a year before when she originally wanted to write the column and crashed Princess Elizabeth's press luncheon. Her tactic of exploiting naive children to promote her career was unethical, but her minor invasion of a public figure's privacy had resulted in the kind of fleeting notoriety that a writer required in their clippings if they wished to get larger projects. She pressed her luck a week later, motivated by the response to her syndicated interview with little Tricia Nixon and spared any criticism for her technique of obtaining it. As she observed the children leaving John Eaton Elementary School in Washington's Cleveland Park area, Jackie could easily have been mistaken for a babysitter or an older sister. She followed the ten-year-old and eight-year-old sisters she had come to see, Ellen and Mamie Moore, nieces of President-elect Eisenhower, out of the schoolyard and onto their short walk home. She approached the trusting girls without introducing herself as a reporter.

"She was wearing a pink suit with high heels," Mamie Moore remembered seven decades later, after catching a glimpse of Jackie out of the corner of her eye in the schoolyard. "She was so beautiful." "I sort of was whispering to Ellen, I told her 'We're not supposed to talk to strangers,'" Mamie continued, as Jackie approached and grabbed their attention, "but then my sister began to talk with her, and then I just joined in."

They were the daughters of Frances "Mike" Moore, Mamie Eisenhower's sister. Jackie engaged them in what appeared to be harmless conversation about how the election had affected their lives. Ellen protested that she only charged fifty cents an hour for babysitting, but "don't you think I should get seventy-five cents now that my uncle is President of the United States?" A girl in my class told me that when my uncle becomes President, I should urge the instructor to give me high grades or he'll kick him off the school board." Her mother informed her, "I could have my birthday there [the White House]," she boasted. I may possibly invite my students to a swimming party."

Little Mamie boasted that she had her photo taken standing between President Truman and Uncle Ike, wearing "some kind of melon pin," and looking "as if I was the most important one." She informed Jackie that her mother had told her that she could take one friend to lunch at the White House, then turned to her downcast friend Carol Jones, who was "still plodding" along behind them, and said she might be the one. Carol "smiled nervously," mumbling under her breath, "I think she's lucky." The presidential niece then brags about her maths skills, calculating that Eisenhower would "have to stay there four terms for me to get married because I don't want to get married for years." "Only three people in my class knew Uncle Ike was my uncle," she was disappointed. Nobody else would believe me. But I have brown hair and bangs, and everyone thinks I look like Auntie Mamie, so now everyone knows."

Little Mamie arrived at the Moore mansion, the site of which Jackie had already pinpointed, hoping that her uncle "won't be so busy being President that he'll forget" to procure her the horse he had promised her.

"Mamie's Namesake, 10, Glad Uncle Ike Will Be President," Jackie's main article, presented the girls as naively humorous, and was accompanied with three of her own hand-drawn cartoon cartoons of Ike and his nieces. It made the top page of the Times-Herald on November 17, 1952, an unusual work given great attention, especially with its drawings rather than photographs. It created a stir in political and press circles, just as Jackie had planned. Most significantly, Jackie had proven her usefulness to the boss once more. Two days after the article was published, Waldrop gave Jackie her first assignment: a full-length feature article about the crowds expected to gather along Pennsylvania Avenue to see Eisenhower, who was on his way to meet President Truman at the White House. It was an enlarged version of the column with narrative context, heavy on interviews. As people gathered in anticipation of seeing Ike, Jackie threaded among them, prodding them to express what they felt he was thinking on this glorious day. It ran on November 19, 1952, with the lengthy headline, "Throngs Four-Deep at White House as Ike Appears: Crowd Kills Long Wait with Speculation." In the coming weeks, Jackie would also land an interview with Pat Nixon, who would inquire who the next chief hostess of capital society would be (Mamie Eisenhower, of course). Five months later, she would interview Richard Nixon himself about the diligence of young pages working in the United States Capitol. Jackie had lunch with her cousin Jack Davis, who hadn't seen her since the summer of 1949, just before she departed for Paris. "I noticed how dramatically she had changed," he recalled, "she seemed much more relaxed, cheerful, and far more beautiful." She now had more freedom, some money in her purse, and was meeting a lot of intriguing people in her job as "Inquiring Camera Girl." He assumed that one reason for the change was the family notion that she had a steady beau, the new senator-elect John F. Kennedy, though she didn't reveal her emotions for him.

In truth, she had not heard from Kennedy since the election. It appears that she did not write or phone him to express her congratulations, but instead waited to hear from him. This was a recurring trend. She would only convey the emotional significance of this to Father Leonard: "He terribly hurt me when he was campaigning and never called up for weeks." And yet, when they were together, he gave her every indication of attentiveness, implying that he cared for her as more than just a friend, to the extent that he was capable of, or willing to, display it. "I think he was as much in love with me as he could be with anyone," she continued to confess to the priest. She knew that if he had remained a bachelor to maintain his appeal to single women voters, he would marry just to suit his political objective after winning the election. "[N]ow maybe he'll want to get married because a Senator needs a wife," she added to Father Leonard. Her anger with Jack's continuous quiet turned into resentment, which she couldn't hide from her cousin. As the meal progressed, she revealed various uncomfortable facts about Jack Kennedy to Davis, including his vanity in constantly grooming his hair to keep it "bushy and fluffy," and his sullen egotism, which manifested itself when "nobody recognizes him or no photographer takes his picture."

Before lunch, however, Jackie made an offhand remark that was not only one of the first confirmations of Jack Kennedy's bigger, concealed plan, but also an admission that she was aware of it.

"Oh, sure, he's ambitious, all right," she said to Davis. "He even said he wants to be President someday."

CHAPTER 14

PALM BEACH, II

Jackie found out a few days after filing her parade piece, her second for the Times-Herald, that the first had jeopardised her employment. Jackie Bouvier had put herself in hot water by making the short three-block walk from the school to the Moore home and continuing to grill the sisters with questions. Frances "Mike" Moore, the girls' mother, was on the phone when they arrived home. It hadn't stopped ringing since the election, and the family would soon need three lines to deal with the unsolicited inquiries now deluging this branch of the incoming presidential family, especially after President-elect and Mrs. Eisenhower came to the house after the parade that Jackie had written about in her second feature article. Mamie said her mother "became immediately very, very upset" when they told her about the ambush interview. Mike Moore phoned her friend George Dixon, who authored the "Washington Scene" column for the King Features syndicate, a few days after the item was published. Dixon was instructed to "do something to make that brash camera girl, whoever she is, know her place." Dixon advised her to phone Waldrop directly, and then quickly informed the editor of her impending call. Waldrop summoned Jackie to interview her about how she came into contact with the youngsters. "stood there, white as a sheet, sure I'd fire her," she said.

He made it obvious to his rogue reporter that what she had done was heinous. Not only had she failed to do her reporter's duty of informing the subjects of her article that she might publish what they'd said, turning trusting children into cartoons, but she had also made them vulnerable to potential kidnapping plots by publishing their school location and home address. When Mike Moore called Waldrop "to complain about the interview," she made it clear that it was taken "without her permission."" She "chewed me out, and in so many words thought I should fire Jackie, and 'How could you keep a reporter with such low tactics at a paper that needs to cover a new presidency?'" Waldrop did not consider it a threat, but he did not know if she had addressed it with the president-elect. It was improbable that Eisenhower would pay attention to such a trivial issue, but as Waldrop put it, "you never know."

Waldrop told Moore that he would take the necessary steps. Desperate to maintain her job, Jackie even suggested that he keep her low-key by allowing her to make illustrations for the paper, attempting to defend the piece and save her reputation by pointing out that her drawings of the Eisenhower nieces were instantly appealing. He assured her he "needed her to do the column" and never considered firing her, but instead put her on "probation" from writing feature articles, lowering her visibility until, as he accurately predicted, Moore forgot about the matter, already swept up in her work on the inaugural committee. Despite this, the chastised columnist remained concerned for her future, stating that the "bad thing right now is that Mrs. Moore is livid." Jackie "told people how sorry she was," Mini Rhea said, noting how her story threatened the Moore sisters: "It must be just terrible to be so prominent that your children are exposed to so much publicity."

Jackie's piece had also sparked interest at the New York Times' Washington bureau. Arthur Krock likely took action after learning the facts of the hardship it had created from Waldrop in order to prevent her from abandoning her literary dreams. He forwarded the clipping to his colleague Bess Furman Armstrong, who had covered First Ladies since Lou Hoover, and suggested she send the young columnist an encouraging message.

Armstrong wrote Jackie, seeing the possibility of turning her story into an illustrated children's book about the White House, narrated by Mamie Moore. Several days before, one of Mummy's friends had sat next to Armstrong during a luncheon. The reporter had regaled the woman with stories from her book White House Profile about presidential families. The friend shared part of the information with Mummy, who informed Jackie. Jackie was enthralled and purchased

Armstrong's book. Jackie was inspired by Armstrong's concept: "[I]f I could only do it correctly. It's so funny—you try to come up with all these amazing, very forced ideas for good children's books—and they never quite gel—and then something so simple comes along—and is the finest of all. That—or anything substantially similar—would never have occurred to me... And now, poor little Mamie Moore, whom I bearded as I walked out of school, might just be my meal ticket." "I can only imagine what she'd say if I called up and said, 'Could I please take Mamie through the White House and write down everything she says?'" Jackie added. I showed Mr. Waldrop your letter, and he knows a woman who is quite close to Mrs. Moore. He stated that in a few weeks, when Mrs. Moore is overjoyed about it, he'll arrange for a buddy to drive me there. Then, if she says I can do it, I'd want to visit you and ask how you think it should be done... I'd hate to mess it up."

Jackie thanked Armstrong profusely for her letter, impressed that she had been a "newspaperwoman all your life." Having the show end with confirmation from such a renowned journalist helped Jackie stay committed to her writing. "I am so in love with all that world now," she said at the end of her November 26 letter. "I think I look up to newspaper people in the same way that you join movie star fan clubs when you're ten years old."

John White's previous attempt to find a publisher for Jackie's book, The Red Shoes, had failed, but she now had a new project in which to invest herself, in addition to the Octagon House documentary. Normally, few barriers stood in the way of pursuing her dreams, but more bad news as the holiday season neared seemed to give her pause. The local CBS affiliate that was about to buy her Octagon House documentary was rescheduling its programming. According to Martha Walter, before the network could manufacture it and pay her for the script, the half-hour program meant to use it "went off the air."

As with gaining the Vogue job after months of hard work only to be forced by Mummy to give it up, fate played against her writing goals once more. Stephen Walter sent her a historical architectural study, Development of the United States Capital, as an early holiday gift on December 3, inscribed "For my hopeful Jackie." Her script would never be produced, despite her excitement about other prospective channels. The letdown, coming so soon after executing an original proposal that almost cost her a columnist job, gave her reason to doubt her instincts. She decided to put the new book idea on hold. Nonetheless, her possibilities at the Times-Herald were set to improve. As the Moore saga faded, there was no doubting that Jacqueline Bouvier was a valuable asset to the company. In a year, she'd turned her column into one of the publication's distinguishing features. Waldrop assigned her a third feature story three days before Thanksgiving. She'd still be in charge of the "Inquiring Camera Girl" section, but he now trusted her to discover and write the longer items she wanted to pursue, as well as to illustrate them with her drawings. In addition to her cartoon sketches of the Moore sisters, she had drawn a souvenir merchant, sailors at a monument, and a housewife who brought her own folding chair to watch the parade. During that holiday season, certain editions of the paper reveal Jackie produced at least one uncredited cartoon for the book review section, featuring a wide-eyed animal—a dog or a sheep—reading a book. In addition, amid the severe summer heat, Jackie had secretly sketched her coworkers attempting to remain cool in the newsroom, hovering around the watercooler, napping on a makeshift bed of several chairs, newspaper covering their faces, feet on the desk. As the holidays neared, she began work on her third film, which was about "shopgirls" in the city's major stores who were seasonal recruits "working the Christmas rush," tasked with wrapping newly acquired items. It was essentially an enlargement of the column style, reliant on capturing dialect and funny situations, as were her two prior pieces. Despite having access to exclusive parties, Jackie Bouvier found the experiences of working people to be more interesting. In the piece, she quoted a clerk who complained about how she was nearly finished wrapping a gift when a customer changed her mind about the gift and paper. "Do you know what makes your feet grow bigger?" another rhetorically said. "Having babies and working during the Christmas rush." Jackie concluded that the gift-wrapping process "made whipping up the Eisenhower Cabinet look like child's play."

She depicted one event with a hilarious cartoon of a worker straining to wrap foam rubber pillows because they "keep popping out and hitting the ceiling," and predicted that the recipient would be scared when she opened it, as if it were a prank snake in a can. The most ridiculous cartoon showed three clerks climbing all over a baby grand piano, attempting to wrap it, with one shopgirl caught in the air when the top flipped open. She closed the story on a touching note, describing a customer presenting a flower bouquet to the cashier for wrapping and asking her to choose wrapping paper and a ribbon she loved. When the gift had been wrapped and paid for, the clerk handed it to the customer, who returned it with the words, "That's for you, Merry Christmas!"

"She had real talent as an artist and a writer," Waldrop would say at the end of 1952, sanctioning a third raise for Jackie Bouvier, up to $56.75 per week ($615 in today's currencies). When combined with her Black Jack monthly stipend, the boost provided her a yearly salary of slightly under $35,000. It didn't put her in diamonds, but with Unk providing her bed and board, it was a substantial sum for discretionary income. Jackie raced to her designer with an idea for a ball gown modified from her imagination rather than any fashion sources. She brought a sketch of a "terrific idea for a dress," as well as eight yards of white satin and two-and-a-half yards of crimson-red velvet and silk. She insisted on "the complete French construction," which included a bra and three layers of taffeta petticoats integrated into the gown. Her design, which cost more than twice her new weekly income, was unlike anything seen in Washington because of one feature: a scarlet stole that flowed over the white gown and all the way down to the floor. It was 45 inches broad at the base. Rhea first displayed it in her workshop, causing other customers to request that she also build them gowns with the "Bouvier stole."

Just before Christmas, an unexpected customer walked in Rhea's clothes boutique with Jackie: Lee Bouvier had returned home for the holidays. Rhea quickly recognized the distinction. Lee was "fundamentally more interested in clothes," according to Mini, and she "always dressed in high fashion" that was "colourful and varied," but lacked Jackie's "continuity," Mini preferring the latter's "less theatrical and more subdued appearance of elegance."

Rhea noticed their opposing personalities even more. Lee "had a grander demeanour than Jackie." Lee didn't say much, didn't share her opinions, and didn't show much interest in me—a little dressmaker. It wasn't that she was nasty; it was just that she lacked Jacqueline's unique warmth." When Rhea said that Lee reminded her of the fashionable but superficial Duchess of Windsor, Jackie "merely smiled."

Jackie was similarly evasive about the shocking news about her sister that was published in national newspapers on December 12, 1952. Lee resigned her job after only nine weeks and became engaged to Michael Canfield, whose father was the president of the book publisher Harper & Row. The era's communal judgement that her younger sister "beat her to the altar" may have generated a sense of inferiority, which was only exacerbated by Jack Kennedy's persistent deafening silence. Jack was a groomsman in his friend Robert Kramer's wedding in Williamstown, Massachusetts, twelve days after his victory. Ten days later, in the last week of November, he went to Europe with Torbert MacDonald, a personal friend and political ally whom he'd known since they were Harvard housemates. Torb was not just Jack's regular companion on abroad vacations where they both womanised with abandon, but he was also a politically ambitious and astute adviser. (In 1954, he ran for and was elected to the United States Congress.) They travelled to England, Ireland, Italy, and France, where Jack met with foreign policy authorities in Paris to discuss the situation in Vietnam. After a three-week absence, Kennedy returned to Boston on December 17 to preside over a children's Christmas party at the VFW named after his late brother. His next trip to Washington was to evaluate candidates for his new Senate staff, not to attend holiday parties with Jackie. The Bouvier stole and gown were viewed on the mannequin rather than on its designer. Yusha had lately informed Jackie that her ex-boyfriend, writer John Marquand, had a successful book. "I'm delighted to hear his book has been chosen as the Book of the Month," he said.

Months before, in a letter to Father Leonard following her July visit to Hyannis, she paraphrased Byron as saying that love is "woman's whole existence," while men kept it aside from their broader public lives. Her instinct that Kennedy saw marriage as a political tool proved right. Jack "wondered about it, whether or not he would have to marry a Massachusetts girl, you know, another Irish girl, that sort of thing," according to Dave Powers. And he waited until he was elected Senator to see whether there was any loss of votes." Jackie Bouvier had not yet realised how mercilessly Jack, Bobby, and the Ambassador would appraise her as a political commodity. She told Gore Vidal that she once overheard them talking about her, and that "they spoke of me as if I weren't a person, just a thing, just a sort of asset, like Rhode Island."

In the weeks following his Senate victory, Jack told several close friends that his father was pressing him to consider running for president. "I think Jack knew the Senate race was the beginning of a long race for the presidency," Charlie Bartlett observed. I believe Joe had the whole thing in his head and Jack was prepared to go." Jackie, on the other hand, was never one of those who thought Jack got resolved to run for president only after winning the Senate and bowing to his father. "I believe he was probably thinking about it for an awfully long time, long before I even knew," she mused. "It was always there."

By the end of the year, she hadn't seen or heard from Jack Kennedy in nearly three months. She had no idea if he had started dating someone else, found some reason to think she was unfit for him, or if there was some unspoken issue behind his inability to move further with their relationship. Initially, she assumed that, like many men, he would have to be persuaded to marry, and her concern was expressed in her column: "How do you expect to get married?" "Did you propose, or were you proposed to?" (I inquired at the marriage licence office.)" "What is your honest take on marriage?" "Can you give me any reason why a happy bachelor should marry?" "What exactly is the food of romance?" "Sean O'Faolain, an Irish author, claims that the Irish are deficient in the art of love." "Are you in agreement?"

"Should girls take advantage of Leap Year?" she wondered in early 1952. She returned to the matter near the end of the year, asking, "What advice would you give a girl who wants to marry before Leap Year is out?" Jackie appeared to accept some of barber Tom Lascola's advice—"Stop waiting for him to propose to you. Propose to him"—and bookkeeper Jean Pievyak, who counselled, "He'll get afraid... just sit tight and wait until next year."

Jackie would not only not propose, but she would also not wait. By the time the senator-elect arrived on December 21, Ambassador Kennedy was already in residence at the family's Palm Beach house, joined by the rest of the family on Christmas Day. Jackie, on the other hand, came to meet his father before Jack arrived. Ralph G. Martin, a historian and former Newsweek editor, left a brief record of a missed episode that seems significant at this vital moment in Jacqueline Bouvier's trajectory some thirty years later. It entailed a "quick and lasting" "mutual affection" between her and the Ambassador, as Martin put it: "She was vacationing with the Auchinclosses at Hobe Sound, and dropped in on the Kennedy home in Palm Beach." There was only the father present. They appeared intent on charming each other, and they succeeded. They went swimming, laughed at each other, and discussed everything from Cardinal Spellman to Gloria Swanson. She had an ally and an admirer when she went."

"I'm more like Mr. Kennedy senior than any other member of his family," Jackie would later note. The British pianist and novelist Robin Douglas-Home, a family acquaintance, claimed that "the only one who really knew her worth from the beginning was Joe Kennedy."

Florida senator George Smathers, a friend and colleague of Jack Kennedy's, subsequently said that Jack "told me that his father told him it was time to get married, and his father preferred Jackie." "Nobody would have talked to Jack at thirty-five that way, including his father," said his more close confidant Lem Billings, especially because Jack "had thousands of girls" from whom he could make his own marital choice. "Mr. Kennedy never let Jack know if the Ambassador was making arrangements to advance Jack's best interests," Billings continued.

Two items appeared in nationally syndicated gossip columns within days of Jackie's visit with the Ambassador alone. According to Aileen Mehle's column "The Gold Coast," which appeared in the December 21 Miami Daily News, "Senator-Elect Jack Kennedy, who is one of the matrimonial catches of the decade, what with being young, intelligent, good looking, rich (but not well groomed), is pretty excited about Mrs. Hugh Auchincloss's daughter Jackie Bouvier, who is young, intelligent, good looking, rich, and very well groomed." On December 23, Dorothy Kilgallen's "Voice of Broadway" column predicted that "U.S. Senator-elect Jack Kennedy and lovely socialite Jacqueline Bouvier will waltz down the aisle early in 1953."

It was the first time Jackie and Jack were mentioned in the press together. Had the Ambassador provided the information? If that was the case, it was not the first time Joe Kennedy had used his extensive network of personal contacts in the press to plant a story about his son's private life without his knowledge in order to further Jack's career.

Jack invited Jackie out on January 3, shortly after the rumour articles linking them were published. He had asked Dave Powers to join them on their first "date" at the Blue Room the previous winter. This time, Jack invited the women on his new Senate staff, Lucy Torres, Jean Mannix, Lois Strode, Mary Gallagher, and Evelyn Lincoln. The "date" was the inaugural session of the Eighty-third Congress, when he would be sworn in as a U.S. senator. They watched, along with his new colleagues and family members, as he was escorted onto the Senate floor—certainly more exclusive company than the thousands of women at the campaign tea party when Jackie had last seen him, but it was still a public event, hardly an opportunity for them to reconnect in a personal way. To emphasise the point, Jack attended an annual New York charity ball three days later with the stunning Maria Carmela Attolico, daughter of the former ambassador to Germany. At the same time, he was chasing Betsy Finkenstadt, the sister of one of Bobby Kennedy's groomsmen, though Lem Billings assumed this was just because "he was never successful in interesting her." When asked if he was "swamped" by marriage proposals from ladies, Kennedy said, "You would think so, but nothing seems to happen."

However, just as he had meticulously planned his long game to win the Senate seat, Jack Kennedy was systematically setting out his preparations for the next significant chapter of his life. And, like Jackie, when the matter was serious, he kept his mouth shut. As a result, when Senator Kennedy asked Miss Bouvier to be his date to the presidential inauguration ball sometime in the first two weeks of 1953, she was completely taken aback.

CHAPTER 15

INAUGURATION

Jackie went out early on January 20, 1953, doing her Pennsylvania Avenue beat from dawn till late afternoon, her sketch pad and reporter's notebook at the ready. She was in town to pen her fourth full-length Times-Herald feature story. She focused her attention once more on the ordinary "folks" who had gathered to see the inaugural parade. Her roaming tale was headlined "Picnic Lunches Help Crowd Wait for Inaugural Parade." She directed her readers to the Pennsylvania Avenue grandstand, from which the Eisenhowers would watch the parade of state floats that followed their open limousines as they left the Capitol. Jackie highlighted the "sleek black Rolls Royces," the "dapper ambassadors," the magnificent state floats, and the celebrities she saw in great detail. Her reporting on these instances was laced with humour, provided not only by the individuals she interviewed, but also by her cartoon sketches of them. One was a man who resembled the board game figure Mr. Monopoly, who was purchasing a hot dog from a street vendor. Another had a Native chief in a headdress who "did a triumphant war dance for the TV camera." A third image showed a Californian member of one of the inaugural parade bands slumped against a tree in Lafayette Square, tired from trekking on the uneven cobblestones of Pennsylvania Avenue. Jackie dashed home to Virginia to prepare for the ball, then back to the city to Kennedy's new house at 3260 N Street in Georgetown, where he was hosting a cocktail party and dinner for Bobby, Ethel, his sisters, and Lem Billings, after fighting her way through the lingering crowds back to the office, quickly filing her story and submitting her ink pen drawings along with it.

Muggsie O'Leary, a former U.S. Capitol policeman who regularly raced Jack to the airport, fetching and delivering packages; George Thomas, an African American Virginia native who served as his personal valet and sometime butler; and Margaret Ambrose, the elderly cook who had begun her association with the family as nanny, were among the family retainers. (Due to his frequent stomach issues, she made sure he ate a consistent diet of what Lem termed "white food," meals with dairy like creamed soups and chicken pot pie.)

With the new year and a new job, Jack had rented the apartment without much thought to its amenities. It wasn't until Ambrose went to start cooking dinner that it was discovered there was no working stove; only a grill was available, thus hamburgers were served at the celebration before the Inaugural Ball. Given that it was new and she had not yet appeared in it, Jackie most likely wore the white gown she had made with the red cape. Before they all went for the ball, Billings motioned for Jackie to join him in another room so they could talk alone. If the subsequent chat offered Jackie her first inkling that she was more than simply one of the senator's girlfriends, it also smacked her with a sharp truth about what she would have to accept if her relationship with Jack Kennedy progressed to the altar. "I told her that night that I thought she ought to realise that Jack was thirty-five years old, had been around an awful lot all his life, had known many, many girls—this sounds like an awfully disloyal friend saying these things—that she was going to have to be very understanding at the beginning, that he had never really settled down with one girl before, and that a man of thirty-five She was really understanding and agreed with everything I said. Of course, I later told Jack what I had said to her—and he was thrilled because he thought it would help her understand him better."

She was gone to the ball before she could absorb the scope of everything Billings implied. There were two inauguration balls, one at the National Guard Armory and one closer to Senator Kennedy's residence, at McDonough Gymnasium on the campus of Georgetown University, which was now adorned with "glittering gold drapes." The Eisenhowers and Nixons arrived at midnight and stayed for an hour, sitting in a balcony above the closely crowded dance floor, with the defeated Henry Cabot Lodge and his wife seated in the box next to them. It was a very formal affair, with men wearing white ties and many women wearing tiaras and orchid corsages. The Howard

University Chorus performed at the ball and other Eisenhower inauguration ceremonies, making them one of the first African Americans to be invited to such occasions. Guy Lombardo's band performed classic dance songs from a previous generation, including "Glow Worm," "Jambalaya," and his signature song, "Enjoy Yourself, It's Later Than You Think."

Despite the fact that Eisenhower had been elected President, the state's new star senator received extensive press in Massachusetts. The Boston Globe wrote the next morning, "Looking a little ruffled and young and affable, Senator John Kennedy was running interference for his sisters, Eunice, Jean, and Patricia." There was no mention of the rest of his party. One "televiewer" in Boston said, having seen him on TV earlier in the day as he filed from the Capitol Rotunda out to the inauguration stand, "He looks like a college kid compared to the others."

There was more coverage of Kennedy, none of it related to his job. From Cedar Rapids to Hackensack, syndicated journalist Inez Robb's readers learned just how popular the new senator was with women of both parties: "He wins the popularity title hands down for the bleak reason that even Republicans have marriageable daughters." And no one in Washington is more qualified than Senator John F. Kennedy. Sen. Kennedy's social and financial standing elevates him above and beyond the call of mere party affiliation. I've seen Republican mothers with their marriageable daughters in the previous several days... with the unscrupulous purpose to snare the junior senator from Massachusetts.... He's so nice and he appears so young that I'm sure women of all ages, including myself, will want to correct his tie, make sure he has a clean handkerchief, and warn him about other women's deceitful ways."

While he and his father disagreed on policy, he had acquired and developed on the Ambassador's media acumen. "If I know one thing," he told his secretary Evelyn Lincoln, "it's that a politician can kill himself faster by playing hardball with the press." I'll chat to them as long as they want to talk to me." Kennedy's cultivation of personal exposure may appear immodest, but it was all for the sake of his political career; in private, his humility was consistent, and he frequently focused attention on others, particularly his most helpless people. Six days after his inauguration, the senator began scheduling regular interviews with reporter Paul Healy for a major Saturday Evening Post biography. During their dinner conversations, Kennedy made no mention of Jackie's existence to Healy. The invitation to the inaugural ball did not imply that their connection would be made public. Jackie was as busy as she'd ever been at the time. She was continually coming up with fresh story ideas and offering them to Waldrop, who was becoming increasingly preoccupied by the paper's difficulties, notably its dwindling revenue. She also attempted to keep the column interesting once the post-inauguration euphoria had subsided. Jack's unexpected celebrity created an instant demand for him as one of the Democratic Party's most popular speakers. He was not only travelling back and forth between Washington and Massachusetts, but he was also venturing further afield. Only a few weeks after being elected, he was chosen to be the keynote speaker at the Jefferson-Jackson Day Dinner in Topeka, Kansas, with former President Harry Truman in attendance—a remarkable performance for a newly elected senator.

Nonetheless, Jackie stated after the inauguration that she and Jack "went out constantly." It was never shown in public. He invited her to infrequent movie outings with Bobby and Ethel, or meals and board games with the Bartletts, but she was the only woman he invited into his family circle. Lem "He started taking her out all the time," Billings agreed. Instead of going out with several various girls, he focused on Jackie."

Evelyn Lincoln's short notations in Kennedy's appointment books are the finest accessible source for the dates and events when they visited each other secretly. Mrs. Lincoln, for example, wrote that he attended the love musical Gigi at the National Theater on Valentine's Day but did not record the name of a guest. While Jack enjoyed going to the movies, he was not particularly fond of musical theatre or anything romantic; given that the theme of Gigi is Parisian society, and given Jackie's fondness for anything related to Paris, Jackie was his likely date. The fact that Jackie's name did not appear in Lincoln's notations, on the other hand, highlighted the unique role she was playing in Jack's life. Lincoln took down the names of other women he met with, such as "Catherine Plummer" (along with other information, a numerical code was included, such as "143, x 754," indicating an apartment number and entry code), while a "Miss Bowen" appointment appeared to be strictly professional and was noted down as being for "a job." Jackie, on the other hand, was set aside. Jack requested that Lincoln contact the other girls he had asked out to supper or the cinema. When Jack needed to see Jackie, he called her directly. "If he was in New York or wherever, he'd say, 'I've got to call Jackie,'" Billings recalled. Normally, he would just phone girls to set up a date." He frequently called her just to talk.

What Billings stated to Jackie at the cocktail party was less an explicit warning about what she should expect if she and Jack agreed to marry and more of a requirement for Jack marrying. Billings added, "Later...," in the same oral history recording in which he remembered pulling Jackie aside. When I brought this up with Jackie again, she responded, "When you discussed it with me, I realised all of that, and I thought it was a challenge." Jackie's allusion to "all that" linked to Lem's statement that Jack was not interested in being monogamous in marriage. This statement indicated that she felt she was up to the task of marrying a man who was almost guaranteed to be unfaithful. Yes, it was the first tangible evidence of Jack's feelings regarding fidelity—but Jackie might have expected that. More than that, it was the first solid proof that Jack was at least thinking about marrying her. Furthermore, Billings presented her with a meaningful revelation that night. Before they even seriously considered marriage, Jack Kennedy wanted Jackie Bouvier to know the truth about himself, which is probably unusual for men who want to be married but are not monogamous; most would want to avoid the danger of losing the potential bride and keep this to themselves. Whatever the classification, what Jack did through Billings can be interpreted as a gesture of respect. He didn't want to hurt her. If she backed away from him for her own good, he would benefit as well.

The earliest proof of Jackie's acquaintance with Kennedy's habits comes from a letter she wrote to Father Leonard in July 1952. She wrote of Jack, "He's like my father in a way—loves the chase and is bored with the conquest—and once married, needs proof he's still attractive, so flirts with other women and resents you."

Black Jack had been open about his own promiscuity with Jackie, even instilling in her the slogan, "All men are rats."

However, by comparing the two Jacks in her life, she would be able to see how dissimilar they truly were.

PART 7

"Become distinct."

—JACKIE'S ADVICE TO HER FRIEND VIVI CRESPI

CHAPTER 16

MEETING OF THE MINDS

He wasn't the candy-and-flowers kind, so every now and then he'd give me a book," Jackie recounted of the times she and Jack seemed to be heading in the same direction. Yusha highlighted "respect for each other's intellect," which they would discover while working together on a range of tasks, as the major conduit through which "love definitely grew."

Furthermore, they had enough in common to get along. She preferred opera and he favoured Irish-American songs, but they both appreciated popular music. Jack ate bland things in tiny servings, while Jackie ate light foods in small portions. Both enjoyed movies and Hollywood gossip. They also had a sharp wit and a fondness for practical jokes. "He liked to make jokes and didn't mind being made fun of... "He enjoyed getting it as much as he did giving it out," a pal recounted. Jackie put that theory to the test several times, including taking Jack out in a rowboat and serving them sandwiches with shaving cream as the filling. When Ethel Kennedy invited her to a St. Patrick's Day party, insisting that all her female guests wear black while she stood out in a bright green gown, Jackie stole the show, arriving late and leaving early in Unk's white Rolls-Royce while wearing a beaded black evening gown shimmering with silver thread, all for Jack's amusement. DURING THEIR PRIVILEGED LIVES, Neither Jack Kennedy nor Jackie Bouvier appeared to truly appreciate the constraints that racism imposed on many Americans. Senator Kennedy did not appear to possess racist views—in all of his recorded private family letters, for example, he never expressed antisemitism, even to his father, who did so publicly in interviews and in his diary—but he frequently appeared oblivious to bigotry.

During his first congressional campaign, his sister Eunice welcomed white volunteer ladies to eat anything they wanted for lunch at a neighbourhood restaurant that was not segregated, but sent sandwiches to the headquarters for Black women volunteers. Aides Hilda Higginbotham and George Taylor were stunned by the gesture, which the latter brought to Kennedy's notice, to which he simply shrugged and muttered, "George, you're thin-skinned." That's one of the things of the period." Despite never being known to utter racial slurs (unlike former President Truman and Senate Majority Leader Lyndon Johnson), Kennedy demonstrated casual bigotry by sending a staff member a Florida postcard picturing an African American guy being terrified by an alligator. Similarly, Jackie once jokingly caricatured a Jewish theatrical agent in a letter she sent when she was young, and another time she created one line of a multi-verse poem in the vernacular of stereotypical southern people of colour. Nonetheless, she was more concerned with uniqueness than Jack. Although she was never advised which specific interviews to print in her column, she included persons of colour of both genders, ages, and occupations. Yusha remembered reading Ralph Ellison's seminal classic The Invisible Man during her first year at the newspaper. Given that homophobia was acceptable in the early 1950s, both of their attitudes toward gay people were more progressive than most. In May 1950, Jackie travelled to Europe with a "effeminate" acquaintance, and she treasured her friendships with Gore Vidal and other men in the arts who were not firmly straight. When Jack was in prep school, Lem Billings sent him a note on toilet paper, which was then used to signify interest because it was easily disposable. "I'm not that kind of boy," Jack politely dismissed. Their emotionally intense bond persisted, and Jackie readily befriended Lem.

Their health was the most major personal difference between them. Jackie had little awareness of her own mortality, despite repeated bad falls from a horse. For Jack, his numerous health issues and near-death experiences impacted not only his sexual drive, but also his attitude and overall outlook on life. It's unknown how much Jackie knew about his physical problems when she first considered him as a potential husband. She was aware of his scarlet fever as a child, and it was already part of his heroic profile that he'd survived being hit by a Japanese destroyer during the war, as well as malaria, which may reappear. His terrible back-muscle ailment became known as a result of his public appearances on crutches. His most dangerous ailment, on the other hand, was only known to his family and doctors. It's unknown when Jackie became aware of the details. After years of perplexing onsets of fatigue, nausea, mood swings, and a skin-pigment change that gave him the appearance of a healthy tan, Kennedy was finally diagnosed with an adrenocortical deficiency, just short of a technical case of Addison's disease, which can be fatal if left untreated. It was eventually treated with liothyronine, a synthetic thyroid hormone, and subsequently cortisone tablets, as well as hydrocortisone, prednisone, fludrocortisone, atropine sulphate, and diphenoxylate hydrochloride, the year before he met Jackie.

With such a damaged endocrine system, he suffered from unforeseen physical collapses throughout the 1945 war, as well as during his 1947 tour to England and 1951 journey to Japan. He was eventually diagnosed with autoimmune polyendocrine syndrome type 2 and moderate asthma. Furthermore, he was initially unable to serve in the armed forces due to one shorter leg, and he was forced to wear a back brace as a result of the complications it produced.

"There were stretches when he was just out of commission," Spalding said. "So that when you saw him or when he came to his friends, he was in a euphoric state, and he was always the best company: so bright, so restless, and so determined to wring every last minute that he just set an abnormal pace." He had this feeling of not being well and wondering how much time he had.... Most of us don't realise how quickly time passes, but he did." In retrospect, John White, for example, saw Jack as "determined to snatch as much pleasure from life as he could in his allotted time." But one of his therapies had a far more significant bodily consequence. Kennedy was once taken methyltestosterone to combat the gonadal atrophy caused by the several drugs, which dramatically increased his libido. If the extent to which Jackie and Jack were sexually involved before marriage remained a private matter between them, so did any financial discussion. Jack treated the subject casually, and there was little evidence that he was concerned that she was after his family's fortune. Money was "something he never really understood." "And he didn't want to," remarked Spalding; "he wasn't interested." He felt no remorse about its origins, no need for more, and was "generous to give what he could." Kennedy never carried a "cabbage" to cover meals, travel, and miscellaneous expenses. He sent invoices to be paid by his family accounts and borrowed money from his buddies so frequently that it became "a standing joke" among them. When George Taylor informed his valet that he owed him $300, he said, "You haven't paid me in four months, so you owe me a balance."

Kennedy revealed to Senate colleague Olin Teague that it was just a few months previously, during the campaign, that he first "became acquainted with a lot of people that were in the low-income group," specifically Boston dockworkers. Despite his vast riches, Kennedy spent very little money pursuing Jackie. They ate at friends' private homes. He frequently didn't have enough money to pay for the few movies they saw on occasion. He didn't buy her anything for Christmas or Valentine's Day. It made the two novels he did acquire for her, The Raven by Marquis James and Pilgrim's Way by John Buchan, all the more unforgettable. They were not chosen at random. He showed how attentive he was to how she thought and her propensity of casting individuals in her life as classical archetypes by handing her both books. The Raven was a Pulitzer Prize-winning biography of Sam Houston, a Texas military and political leader who helped build the state's independence, and one of Jack's idols. Author Marquis James employed meticulous research, colourful prose, and dramatic narration to enliven Houston as the protagonist among a galaxy of other Lone Star State heroes, as he had done in his biographies of Benjamin Franklin, Andrew Jackson, and Woodrow Wilson. The publisher even referred to the book as "legendary stuff." Jackie preferred her history to be meandering and lively, rather than a bloodless academic study of how one person might lead a movement and symbolise a period. It's easy to imagine Jack giving her the book as a glimpse into how he wished to be remembered in history. Pilgrim's Way was published by John Buchan about his successful career as a British diplomat, which included serving as Canadian governor general. His writer and historian instincts merged in his profiles of notable English politicians ranging from King

George V to Raymond Asquith, the latter being one of Kennedy's heroes. Reading had been a safe haven for Jack and Jackie since childhood, protecting them from the miseries of a terminal illness and a bitter divorce. They liked literature set in or set in early-nineteenth-century England. Among Jack's favourite books was David Cecil's Melbourne, which told the story of British Prime Minister Lord William Lamb Melbourne and his unconventional marriage to novelist Caroline Ponsonby, who was also the lover of poet Lord George Gordon Byron, whom she described as "mad, bad, and dangerous to know." Byron, Jackie's favourite author, had sexual affairs with everyone from a half sister to cousins to other men. Shakespeare was another shared interest. She was taken with Jack's ability to quote from his works "out of the blue." "He knew all the great speeches and the problems of every man in those plays," she said of Jack, who favoured Henry V and Richard III.

It wasn't just what they read, but also how voraciously they read, that became a point of familiarity. "Jackie's mind was like a sponge," one of her pals recounted. She likes to read numerous novels at once and set a timetable for herself to finish them all." Billings noticed the similar trait in Jack. "His entire mind could completely concentrate on what he was reading, and he would block out the rest of the world.... [H]e was always reaching for something to read." "Jack did not write poetry," Jackie subsequently remarked, in contrast to herself. But he always reads it to me alone."

It was incorrect to credit Jackie's ambitions to the formal education that privilege provided her; most of her peers from the top class who were similarly educated (including her sister) were unmotivated to develop themselves or use their intellect to strive for higher callings. Jackie was ecstatic to notice this resemblance in Jack: "He had, which I think he gave himself," she remarked. He was shaped by the Greeks, Romans, and British. All of this he discovered in his own private reading."

Both knew that intelligence was not derived solely from reading. It was critical to have intuition about individuals, the masses, and the truth of a stated circumstance. That came from getting out and about and mingling with others. Both drawn to seclusion, they made an effort to take their gaze away from the page. Jackie insisted on not being labelled as a "bluestocking... because I'm not." People are much more important to me than literature. I'd rather participate in life than withdraw from it like a professor." She saw Jack in a similar light, feeling that he was "full of love—for life... for the great adventure of politics and... what he knew had to be done... for all the things that nourish his body and spirit," as well as "love for me."

"We both have curious, inquiring minds," she remarked subsequently simply as the reason "we chose each other." She discovered in Jack what she had told Frank Waldrop about herself when he originally inquired what she wanted to write about at the paper; he was "interested in everything." She also realised how, having lived a dozen years longer than she had, Jack could help her think more clearly. In her words, he was "not romantic, but idealistic." For one thing, she discovered he assisted her in "thinking objectively." Other distinctions were significant. "I make ghastly snap judgments of people," she wrote to Yusha. "I don't think Jack Kennedy ever made a snap decision about anyone," Lem noted. After hearing his ideas on how to address national challenges, she came to refer to Jack as "the man who made me a Democrat."

But he was also curious about what she knew. She was particularly taken by the way he'd ask what she was reading and then pick up her book when she put it down. "When I studied French literature, he went right along with me."

In terms of Jackie's French ability, Jack had a more ambitious plan than simply having her translate letters from his French-Canadian voters. He had more books for her in the early spring of 1953, she recalled, about a dozen abstruse, laborious studies, thick with information about the dismal aspects of the French war in Indochina, and all written in French. At the same time as he was dealing with more pressing issues of commerce and trade for Massachusetts, Kennedy began to focus on Indochina. Since his late 1951 journey to Vietnam, during which he met with both French and Vietnamese authorities, Kennedy had not lost sight of the importance of granting the country freedom in name as well as actuality. On February 18, he met with the Vietnamese ambassador in the morning. He talked with Ed Gullion, a former US ambassador he met in Saigon, who agreed that American backing for France was merely maintaining the West's colonial grasp on a nation of people who were beginning to despise and turn against it. He hired Priscilla Mullins, a Harvard graduate and international affairs expert, to mine all of Gullion's findings on the subject for a report. He had the most stringent duty for Jackie. He needed her to read all of the books and figure out which passages were pertinent to his goal. She would then translate them from French to English and compile them all into one final report. The study has to include the history of the French in Indochina from colonisation to the present day, including all official treaties. The assignment's completion has enormous stakes. It would boost the senator's reputation on foreign policy, as well as Jackie's own future with him. It was a significant request. It made her think. "One of my most annoying flaws is getting very excited about something at the start and then tiring of it halfway through," she revealed two years ago. I'm attempting to counteract this by not becoming too excited about too many things at once."

Jackie, who was always drawn to what was most difficult, couldn't help but take it joyfully. The fact that Jack Kennedy requested her to do it, as well as the opportunity to demonstrate the power of her mind, made it attractive. It enabled her to let go of any self-imposed limitations on her knowledge and abilities, as well as her anxieties of being classified as unfeminine and hence uninteresting. It proved Jack to be the only man she'd ever had who treated her with intellectual respect. If she "thought" she was in love with Jack Kennedy in July 1952, the full flush of that passion must have bloomed alongside the spring blossoms in April 1953. Most importantly, by entrusting Jackie with presenting a fantastic report on Vietnam, he implied his willingness to accept her into the type of serious partnership she desired. Such a collaboration would be the adventure of a lifetime, a life vast enough to utilise not only her writing abilities but all of her talents. Jackie would subsequently adopt Jack Kennedy's concept of "happiness" as her own: "complete use of one's faculties along the line of excellence and a life affording one's scope." By ending her engagement to the traditional Husted in 1951, Jackie defied the usual assumption that she had to choose between being a wife and being a working woman; by 1953, she was able to foresee what had previously seemed impossible: a unique blend of both alternatives.

The Vietnam project Jack wanted Jackie to take on was the type of endeavour he may have taken on himself. His love of writing began in college, when he authored a thesis that was redrafted into Why England Slept, which was published when he was twenty-three years old. It demonstrated his adherence to what one of his biographers called "unsentimental realism" and "clear headed and informed calculation" in confronting such challenges. However, by 1953, his writing was narrowed to events "in which he had participated" or "about which he had some firsthand knowledge," according to Spalding; he "began to write as a politician... involved in political events." His time as a journalist from April to August 1945 had taught him the significance of succinct yet descriptive writing.

Nobody would have guessed from Jackie's Times-Herald work that she could create the kind of report Kennedy desired, but he knew her well enough to believe she could. By April 1953, it also appears likely that he would have realised that they shared the same human rights ideals, which were crucial to Kennedy's evolving foreign policy ideas. The idea of what he was looking for and what she eventually provided appeared to be similar to that of Why England Slept, but it was not meant for publication but rather to serve as the foundation for his first significant Senate foreign policy speech.

Kennedy was betting his national—and eventually international—reputation on becoming an Indochina expert, which would help him make the case that he was qualified to lead the United States itself. However, it was not a sham political scheme. The events in Indochina struck at the heart of his belief in the right of a people to self-determination.Jackie's employment did not require her to analyse foreign-aid budgets. She was not asked to evaluate troop and armament budgets. It was simpler, but more significant. It was based on the world of words that she and Jack inhabited and knew the power of. She agreed to take on the task.

"Once you have the ability to express yourself, you can tell the world what you want from it," Jackie would later say. "All changes in the world, for good or ill, were initiated by words."

CHAPTER 17

THE VIETNAM REPORT

She was back at it, nestled away in the seclusion of her favourite private writing spot, up in her modest room at Merrywood, with the huge window that looked out across the meticulously manicured grass toward the river. Jackie, on the other hand, was in the streets of Saigon and the rice fields near Hanoi in her mind.

Jackie began work on what would become her eighty-four-page report on France's political, military, economic, and social grip over its Indochinese colony of Vietnam in late March 1953. It was the focus of a research file Jack was putting together, the cornerstone of his in-depth investigation.

She began the task on her own, while also managing the Merrywood household for a portion of the time. On January 28, Mummy and Unk flew to Lebanon to visit Yusha, who was ready to work for an American oil business. Mummy admitted that being away was "nerve-racking" because Lee's wedding was scheduled for the day after she returned, on April 18.

Kennedy required a massive quantity of factual data to present to the Senate an airtight argument opposing prolonged American backing for France's war against Communist insurgents in Vietnam's north. Any work Jackie had started on her children's book about the White House was put on hold. The Vietnam report—her new "spring project"—was diametrically opposed to the Octagon House documentary and the Vogue columns. "He gave me all these French books and asked me to translate them," she would recollect more than a decade later. And I was living alone at my mother's house in Virginia, working for the Times-Herald. And I'd stay up all night translating these books.... I think I translated maybe ten." She cited two books: one about French admiral Georges d'Argenlieu, the colonial administrator of Indochina from 1945 to 1947, and another about independence leader Ho Chi Minh and the Ammonites, the ancient tribal peoples of central Vietnam. In her final report, she primarily relied on Philippe de Villiers' Histoire du Vietnam from 1940 à 1952.

According to a cover note from Ernest S. Griffith, the Library of Congress legislative reference service director, dated April 20, 1953, Kennedy requested further resources, which could have been the "articles on contemporary French politics" that he later asked her to describe.

There was nothing confidential about the material or his need for it, therefore Kennedy did not seek the assistance of any government or professional translators to accomplish even a portion of the job. "Yeah, he could read French," Jackie later admitted, "but not well enough to put his trust in himself for a lot of facts and things." The fact that he asked Jackie to do the work suggests that he wanted her to do it because she shared his vision of an independent Vietnam, as seen by her final report.

Jackie's first concern was not her linguistic ability, but rather that "I couldn't tell what was important and what wasn't," and that she was "really sort of skimming through the pages." The study required a precise blend of historical chronology and analysis, which meant she had to sift through the materials, assess what information was relevant, perform "translation" of key parts, and then intricately combine everything into a logical, structured document.

She clearly stepped up to the plate. The final report opened with an eighteen-page typed, double-spaced essay describing the French in Vietnam's history, from colonisation to the most current developments in the war. She evidently pecked it out herself, based on her own admission of being a bad typist and the fact that the part was not properly typed. Perhaps because she despised typing, the rest of her report was handwritten in her clear, distinct calligraphy, and it was astounding for the minor yet crucial data she included, as well as its sixty-six-page length. The work as a whole demonstrates her keen understanding of human nature and her ability to reconcile objectivity with sensitivity.

Jackie separated the typed text into three sections. Part I began with the 1860 Franco-British expedition to Indochina and ended with the French forcing out the Japanese occupation as World War II came to a close. Parts II and III chronicled the postwar years, culminating with the defeat of Bao Dai, the emperor of Annam, Vietnam's centre region spanning roughly two-thirds of the country.

The handwritten first section of Jackie's report is a detailed examination of five significant deals reached between France and Indochina between March 1945 and June 1948. Her concluding statement, "Cost of Vietnam War," was perhaps the most informative and convincing aspect of the report. This appears to have been her personal opinion, set apart from the factual evidence and shocking in its humanism, and it would turn out to be prescient. Jackie saw the situation as a conflict between the French and the Viet Minh, "each fighting for power." "What's the point of the fight if neither side wins?" she asked, seeing the absurdity of the situation.

When condemning the power struggle, Jackie frequently referred to the Vietnamese people who were being exploited by it: "They want a new way of life—no foreign domination, no corrupt mandarinate.... It is to them that we must hand over the reins." She ultimately placed the onus on France, which had published declarations recognizing Vietnamese independence, saying that "[s]he should now follow up her words with actions—in letting the people freely choose their own destiny." In addition to the fact that France had lost 30,000 men and its economy had been harmed, Jackie claimed that the French government had been deceiving its citizens: "Propaganda makes this look like a defensive war when it's really a conquest," and the French government "exploits patriotic sentiment to justify a misguided policy." Peace, she added, would come only when Vietnam's people trusted their leaders, but "[i]t's not for the French, Chinese, or Americans to say who those people are."

While she slammed the Soviet and Chinese authorities and their goals in Vietnam, Jackie refused to accept that an independent Communist Vietnam would simply become a puppet of another state. "Nothing has proved that a communist [nation] in Asia is automatically dominated by the Kremlin and closed to all other influences," she claimed.

Jackie was well aware of the dangers to any public figure who advised keeping an open mind about Communism as she wrote her report, having asked in one of her "Inquiring Camera Girl" pieces, "If you secretly found out you had married a former Communist, what would you do?" She occasionally used the column to elicit feedback on features of the Soviet system and the Cold War ("If you could send a message behind the Iron Curtain, what would you say?"). "Would Stalin's death help or hurt world peace?" "Do you agree with Malenkov that all differences between Russia and the United States can be resolved peacefully?" "What four Americans would you nominate as United Nations delegates to match Russia's team of Vishinsky, Gromyko, Zorin, and Zorubin?" But what she said in the report may be interpreted as direct—and dangerous. On the document's concluding page, Jackie openly stated her own opinion based on what she had learned and grown to think, daring Kennedy "to say in your speech that we should give Indochina to the communists because they are the ones with the most integrity!"

Despite the sombre matter, her final sentence on the last page demonstrated her wit: "END—Thank heavens."

The behind-the-scenes project had been a time-consuming, taxing, and yet enlightening endeavour, thoroughly immersing Jackie in the nuances of military strategy and leaving her with a better understanding of present world affairs. It brought her full circle from

Pierre Renouvin's Sorbonne class, whose intellectual opinion on the futility of France regaining authority over the Vietnamese had been burnt into her consciousness. In 1951, the concept of autonomy was personal for her, as she sought to escape Mummy's and, to a lesser extent, Black Jack's dominion over her every thought and decision. After studying the philosophy behind it, her foundational conviction in self-determination freedom became a core principle in 1953. Jackie had addressed Indochina with Yusha when he visited her in Europe in June 1950, and again the following year as she read books by André Malraux that dealt with the colonial quandary. A letter Yusha addressed to her on December 18, 1952, demonstrates that they were conversing about a similar worldwide scenario at the time. While in Beirut, he had been researching the "Palestinian problem," as well as reading the Koran and St. John Philby's Arabian Days. He spoke to her about the effects of colonial dominance in the region. "A people so long subjected, extremely diverse, not well educated historically," he wrote to her, "when... desperate, [are] easily swayed by mob force and communism." But they, like us, believe in fundamental human and social rights... of liberty, individuality, the integrity of what they cherish, and the right to self-defence."

The opinions and facts in Jackie's report caused Kennedy to call his friend Thurston Morton, assistant secretary of state, and ask numerous and detailed questions concerning the United States' assistance for France in Indochina. He was curious as to how much funding the US government was supplying. He inquired whether the French had a "success plan" in Indochina—"military, economic, and political." He wondered how the French intended to obtain Vietnamese backing, whether any agreements could be amended, and to what extent the various factions had accepted them. Kennedy's questions, according to Morton, "cover so many aspects of this subject" that it would take "several days to furnish the information." After more than two weeks of silence, Jack wrote a sharp letter to Secretary of State John Foster Dulles. "While I was aware that it would require considerable research and extensive preparation," he wrote, the eager freshman senator demanded answers "at your earliest convenience." The answers he received were evasive and ambiguous, creating a red flag for Kennedy as he proceeded. Jackie's report made a strong case for France to grant Vietnam independence, bolstering the argument that Jack had already articulated during his December 1951 visit to Indochina, that it was necessary in "support of the legitimate aspirations of the people of this area against all who seek to dominate them—from whatever quarter they may come." As he learned how attentive Jackie could be to the complexity already at work in Indochina, Jack's intuition that her beliefs and principles would make her an ideal partner grew stronger. She agreed after presenting her report to the senator.

"After all I have done for him," she reflected eleven years later, "he has got to ask me to marry him."

CHAPTER 18

DATING

As Easter weekend, the first weekend in April, neared, Jack Kennedy conscientiously ensured that his whole crew would be taking those days off, then left on Thursday, April 2, to spend the vacation with his family in Palm Beach. He sent Jackie a hibiscus flower postcard with the message, "Wish you were here." Jackie later claimed that it was his only written confession of love during their courtship. (She missed a telegram he sent just over a month later, leaving her with only two known love notes from him.

However, Jack was making overtures to her in other ways, and she was accepting them. While she was hesitant to reveal information about her dating life, she and Jack were both becoming more at ease with others knowing they were "involved." Charlie Bartlett was one of the few people with whom she related stories of her escapades with Jack, telling him how, on one occasion, she'd secretly arrived at his office to "kidnap" the senator for a limited period of time, transporting him to the Glen Echo amusement park. Despite the growing frequency of Jack and Jackie's dates, the senator, according to Charlie, remained committed to his major passion: politics. "One thing at a time," he explained to Charlie. Even his closest friends were unaware that Jack was considering marriage. "No, he just never talked about it," Spalding replied. "He was having... success in whatever he did, and he was moving along... quickly enough for himself.... He wasn't bothered by the fact that he wasn't living a connubial life." He also professed to be opposed to what he considered as typical romantic conduct, telling historian James McGregor Burns, "I'm not the heavy romantic type." The good news was that Jackie was also reluctant to completely express her sentiments, making them a suitable match. If Kennedy had been overly emotional, it would have bothered her. Jackie's friend Lorraine Shevlin, who was dating Kentucky Senator John Sherman Cooper at the time, remembered how she commiserate with Jackie about how much time the guys put in at work. "We said... how terrible it must be to be married to a politician... it was all sour grapes because neither senator had asked us to marry him at that point." Lorraine, a divorcee, advised Jackie, "Should your husband feel compelled at some point to cheat on you, either cheat back or buy yourself a diamond tiara and send him the bill."

Jack tried to balance his personal and professional lives, but when he took Jackie out to dinner with an adviser or buddy, she was sometimes irritated and occasionally left the table. Others seemed to assume she had nothing to say, unlike Dave Powers at their first supper, who had asked her what she felt about Jack's Senate run. As tape recordings of chats with journalists who joined them for dinner show, she eventually volunteered her insights if she thought the others were trustworthy pals. In general, whatever political counsel or views she supplied Jack would be tightly limited to private conversations or written correspondence between them. Jackie's Vietnam report established the precedent. On the other hand, Kennedy began to appear more eager to prioritise her over his careful PR generation. He'd cancelled a dinner meeting with Paul Healy, who was nearing the end of their interviews for the Saturday Evening Post article, to instead take Jackie out, as recorded in his business calendar with what looks to be his own handwritten notation of "Bouvier."

Simultaneously, Jackie began assisting his career by exposing him to her own tiny but considerable network. Esther Unk, Unk's sister, was married to Norman Blitz, a prominent Nevada developer and fundraiser with major political connections in the West; Blitz and his affluent cronies would be vital to Jack in future races. Jackie assisted Jack in establishing a close friendship with her Newport friend Claiborne Pell, who was then a State Department Foreign Service officer. "I met Jacqueline first," Henry Brandon, the London Sunday Times Washington bureau head, recalls. "It was through her that I met him, was welcomed to her house, and gradually got to know him more.... It was more of a social interaction at first than a relationship between a newspaperman and a politician."

Such advances, combined with her Vietnam report, heightened Jack's interest in this woman who, as he later told their mutual friend Joan Braden, "could really think like a man, rational and had acute insight." (The compliment was sexist, but it was popular at the time.) Yusha also said Jack was intrigued by Jackie's "inquisitive, no-nonsense mind" and was realising "how much... he needed her advice and her kind of comfort." Even if Jack avoided asking Mary to marry him, Lem Billings saw the inevitable. "I could tell Jackie was different from the other girls Jack had dated right away." "She was smarter, more literary, and more substantial," he observed. "They were soul mates. Jack and Jackie are two parts of one whole."

Still, as the weeks passed, Jack made no concrete suggestions. And, while Jackie had been thinking about marrying Jack for nine months, she had also been thinking about how her sense of self might be compromised by a life in national politics and being integrated into the Kennedy family; whether researching and writing for the senator would be worth sacrificing her pursuit of a professional writing career (and how often he would call on her anyway, given that he had a staff to research and write for him); and, of course, how her sense of self might be compromised by being integrated into the Kennedy family. Her initial reaction to Billings' presentation of Jack's condition for marriage had been to characterise it as a challenge she was up to, but based on other remarks she made, Jackie hadn't given up hope that marriage could transform Jack. She even advised a friend that guys were "always surer to last if they sow their wild oats first." Nonetheless, she had heard and seen enough of Black Jack to know that no wife could change a determined adulterer's behaviour. The only thing that could be changed was a wife's acceptance of it. Jackie was vehemently opposed to divorce, according to multiple families. The task was not to alter an adulterous husband, but to govern herself in response to him. She never forgot how, as she told Father Leonard in July 1952, Black Jack's infidelity "nearly killed Mummy." Even still, she felt that Janet's actions would never be justified.

"She was going to make sacrifices in order to be a political wife," Yusha thought. "[S]he would not have permitted divorce." The Catholic Church barred divorce even in circumstances of infidelity; no divorced Catholic could be elected president; and Jack Kennedy was determined to become the first Catholic president. Jackie pointed out in a handwritten draft of a remark that appears to have been either an homage to Joe Kennedy or a submitted contribution to Rose Kennedy's future memoirs that the benefit of Jack's Catholicism was that their children "would learn that marriage is permanent." In stating that she would always "thank his father" for giving the example for Jack's "sense of family," one can't help but notice the irony she may have intended: Jack's marital model was the Ambassador, who never divorced his wife despite his infidelity. Janet and Lee had both expressed reservations about Jack being a good fit for Jackie. Janet, according to Jack, "has a tendency when she's excited to think I'm not good enough for her daughter and talks too much—talks just too much." "I kept him company while he waited for her and didn't make his visit a bit pleasant because I didn't think he was paying Jackie enough attention," Lee said one evening when Jack came to pick up her sister for an evening out. I just wanted him to know that no one was suitable for her."

Lee and Michael Canfield's wedding was set for Saturday, April 18, with the ceremony at Georgetown's Holy Trinity Church and a reception at Merrywood. The night before, Unk and Mummy arranged a supper for the wedding party at the F Street Club, with guests from the Canfield, Lee, and Auchincloss families. The Bouviers and Black Jack were not invited. Her father did attend the ceremony the next day, arriving by train in the morning with his sister Michelle and her husband, as well as her twin, Maude, who insisted on attending despite her alienation from her brother. At the ceremony, Black Jack arrived, facing his ex-wife and her second husband's undeniable wealth, to accompany his younger daughter down the aisle. As maid of honour, Jackie donned "ballerina-length bouffant gowns of yellow chiffon, veils of yellow tulle attached to circles of fern and carried bouquets of fern," as Nini recalled. Kennedy was in Massachusetts the weekend and was unable to attend. The bride tried to be witty in thanking guests for their gifts at

146

the spring celebration in Merrywood's sylvan setting, but the sarcasm was clear. "How did you guess that what Michael and I wanted more than anything else on earth was a pair of carving knives with china handles?" she asked one of the guests. "It seems a shame to ruin such lovely things with meat." "I believe we'll just use them on each other when we're angry." Louis Auchincloss remembers Black Jack "dancing Janet around when she didn't want it at all." We assumed he'd take Janet with him."

Jackie appeared to be blissfully unaware of the family conflict. She solicited comments from ushers for inclusion in her column, joking that if they didn't comply, she'd make up their response. "But Jackie, what is the question?" one person inquired. "I'll make up the question, too!"

Despite her cheerful attitude toward the column, she was becoming frustrated at work. Jackie was losing interest in coming up with interesting column questions six days a week, and her goal of moving completely to feature articles remained unmet. She'd only completed four movies in about a year and a half on the job by April 1953. She began to wonder if she had selected the appropriate place for her work. "She insisted she would be a writer for the rest of her life, but she grew tired of doing it for a newspaper," Yusha would recall.

In some ways, she was a victim of her own success, having made the "Inquiring Camera Girl" so distinct to the Times-Herald brand that Waldrop encouraged her to stick with it. She'd become accustomed to his dismissing her requests for feature assignments, but she was also upset that the time required to perform the column well stopped her from developing and proposing a larger number of full-article ideas. What she didn't realise was that the Times-Herald had continued to lose money, and Waldrop was trying to cut overhead costs or face the potential of the owners having to sell the publication at a loss. Jackie's column questions at the time revealed her displeasure with her employment and her supervisor ("Does your job require you to use your highest abilities?"). "Would you like to be the boss here, and if so, what would you change?" "What subject in school has been the least useful to you now?" "What is your secret ambition?"

She had reached a breaking point, telling society reporter Angela Gingras, "I am going to quit this job." "Not only did she feel that the newspaper was exploiting us—we were being overlooked and underpaid—but there was a sense of personal indignation," Gingras explained. Jackie knew that the editors saw her as a Junior League member, useful but not necessary. They dismissed her because she wasn't covering breaking news."

Finally, Waldrop brought her into his office one morning in April 1953 to offer her a job that would combine her professional and personal lives. Despite the fact that it was for a column rather than a feature, it had the potential to garner national attention. He requested her to do interviews with some of the country's most well-known senators, all of whom he knew personally. He provided her a list of candidates, including North Carolina Democrat Clyde Hoey, Nevada Democrat Pat McCarran, Ohio Republican Robert Taft, and Utah Republican Wallace Bennett. Jack Kennedy was the youngest and newest senator on his list. Waldrop was aware that Jackie had been "seeing" Kennedy, and he couldn't help but speak up before she departed to express his paternal concerns. He told her that many other ladies, "a whole generation ahead of you," had become heartbroken over Jack Kennedy's death, and counselled her, "You behave yourself." Don't get too excited. He's too old for you, and he doesn't want to marry." She "rolled her eyes, said nothing, and went off on her assignment," he said.

The column would be distinctive in another way, shaped by the nature of the odd question, in that it would contrast each elected official's reaction with that of the young Senate page messengers. "How is it like observing the pages up close?" the senators were asked. "How is it like observing senators up close?" the pages were asked. It's unclear if Waldrop or Jackie devised the dual set of questions, but it seems likely that it was Jackie, given that she was in on the inside joke within Jack's circle that he resembled a college intern rather than an elected person. Jackie also got a surprising scoop and a sixth interview. After she'd interviewed Jack, he brought her to the country's most powerful man: Vice President Richard Nixon. As freshman members of Congress in 1947, Kennedy and Nixon became friends. Their offices were immediately across the hall at the time, and when the California Republican ran for Senate against Democrat Helen Gahagan Douglas in 1950, Jack walked a $1,000 contribution from Nixon's campaign to him. Jackie had now interviewed all four members of the Nixon family by sitting down with the vice president. Meanwhile, Jackie's assignment to interview Jack in the Times-Herald newsroom fanned murmurs about their connection into loud talk. Some of Jackie's female coworkers were envious. "We were all young women, most of us unmarried, and everybody wanted to get assignments to talk to young Jack Kennedy," Agnes Ash, a women's page writer, remembered. "Everyone knew that whoever married him would become the first lady one day." It was a foregone conclusion."

\Soon after, Jack arrived at the Times-Herald office to see Jackie. One long-circulated story among the Times-Herald building's personnel and tenants was that the senator arrived in a cab, ran into the newsroom, located Jackie, and asked her for money to pay the driver. She spewed it up. He remembered visiting Inga Arvad and his sister Kathleen in the newsroom a decade before. The senator grew slightly uneasy when Waldrop joked about his earlier days with Inga. Waldrop spotted Jackie "rolling her eyes" yet again. Jackie did not let the fact that she was now dating Jack Kennedy detract from her objectives. The essay based on conversations with senators and the vice president provided a humanising portrait of these guys with otherwise distant public personas. She appears to have impressed Waldrop enough that he agreed to recast it as a longer piece, and she excitedly wrote to a literary agent, identified only as Mrs. McCrea in the only surviving letter Jackie wrote on Times-Herald letterhead, that "[t]he editor liked it so much that we are now going to run it as a Sunday feature." I hope you think it's okay.... I'll let you know when the piece will be live as soon as the other [interviews] arrive. Thank you very much for your thoughtfulness—and please ignore the pencil. I'm a bit slow on the typewriter—and there doesn't seem to be a pen at a newspaper office." Little is known about why Jackie contacted the literary agent, aside from Waldrop's vague recollection that his columnist had an idea for a young-adult book about the Senate, an angle perhaps inherent in her interviewing the pages or prompted by an earlier idea for a children's book about the White House. Whatever the reason, the item was written as a regular column rather than a feature on Tuesday, April 21, and did not become a book. It felt like she was at a crossroads in her career life as well as in her relationship with Jack. She was becoming as disillusioned with his ambitions to marry her as she was with her career. Later, she told a friend that she was wondering "if I'll live long enough to marry him."

Aileen Bowdoin (Bow's older sister) had recently divorced and returned to live with her mother and stepfather, Emily and Ed Foley. On Saturday, May 16, the Foleys surprised Aileen with a birthday celebration because she was "having a tough time." At the party, Aileen's mother "announced that she thought it would be fun if I took a trip to Queen Elizabeth's coronation, which I must say was the last thing in the world that I would have done." 'Okay, Mom, I'll go [but] I'm not going unless I have someone to go with me because I'm not going to go over and take on the Queen by myself,' I said. So I called Jackie and asked if she wanted to go. "It was probably Monday when she said, 'I'll let you know tomorrow.'"

Mummy then got in on the act, first hearing about it via Emily Foley, and confronted Jackie with her reasons for why she wanted to go because "I felt she really needed it." According to Janet's account, her elder daughter felt bad about herself after her younger sister married first, and she was "awfully tired... working for the Times-Herald all winter." Janet further said that she "suspected" Jackie's original opposition to the trip was due to her reluctance to leave Jack Kennedy, "although she had never really said so because she is the sort of girl who covers her feelings." Janet chastised her, telling her that if Jackie was "doing exciting things instead of sitting here waiting for the phone to ring," Jack "would be much more likely to find out how he felt about you."

Jackie was eager to leave, but for the opposite reason Janet had indicated. The vacation, in her opinion, could be "a chance to do some regular writing." She told Aileen that flying to England and attending the coronation could help her get many feature articles published in the Times-Herald. When she approached managing editor Sidney Epstein about flying to Europe on Tuesday, he initially assumed she wanted a paid three-week vacation and refused. His mood altered when she told him she was going to the coronation. Aileen stated, "[S]he had gone to the editors to see if she could get assignments covering the events." "We had been trying without success to get someone into the coronation," Epstein revealed. I told her, 'Go! But you must write us letters that we will airmail back. Every day, include a sketch." She renewed her passport on Wednesday, May 20, describing her occupation as "photographer."

Janet paid for the vacation, according to subsequent biographies. Mummy claimed Jackie told her that "if they [the Times-Herald] don't want to, I'd like to give you the trip," but Aileen testified that "Jackie insisted on principle that the paper cover her travel and hotel if she was going to be writing stories for them—or else she refused to go." According to Aileen, the Times-Herald agreed to reimburse Jackie for the majority of her London vacation with a small stipend, and she "saved every receipt." In truth, Jack Kennedy already knew how he felt about her; shortly before she departed Washington, he broached the subject of marriage. According to Jackie's friend Joan Braden, one night before her departure, Kennedy abruptly ceased vacillating. "[H]e wanted to get married and didn't want to get married," Braden explained, "and then she told me about the night he finally got married." And so she went to the coronation."

However, saying he "finally did" want to marry one night shortly before she departed was not the same as asking her to marry him.

Aileen Bowdoin, who was in Jackie's constant presence for the following two weeks and five days, confirmed this, claiming that "[h]e had asked her about marriage." Billings frequently said for the record in his early comments on the subject, "Jackie, to my knowledge, was the only female he ever wanted to marry.... Except for Jackie, Jack Kennedy never proposed to anyone." When asked if the senator had asked Jackie Bouvier to marry him, even Lem conceded, "I wasn't actually that sure." In a later interview, he elaborated: "I couldn't imagine him actually saying 'I love you' to someone and asking her to marry him." It was the kind of thing he would have preferred to happen without having to discuss it."

Regardless, Jack's estimates appear to have shifted. He had waited until he believed it was important to marry, and that time had come. "It wasn't until he had presidential ambitions that he felt marriage was a necessity," Billings went on to say. "I believe he had reached the point where he felt it was politically important to marry—fortunately, Jackie arrived at the right time."

Accounts that portray Kennedy as using Jackie to further his goals omit the fact that she sought to use him to further her own. "She wanted the White House just as much as he did," her friend Tish Baldrige claimed simply. "She aspired to be the country's First Lady." Louis Auchincloss stated that Jackie's goal justified her willingness to wait so long for a marriage proposal, adding plainly, "Jackie had always known exactly what she wanted, and how to get it." Even Yusha revealed she shared Jack's presidential aspiration, though he couched it in loftier terms, stating they were "both very patriotic people" with a "great sense of duty."

"I wanted Jack to be President," Jackie explained to a friend. "You don't often recognize greatness when you're up close to it—but I did, and I wanted him to save my country."

A long-term presidential bid was, according to Bartlett, "really part of the deal going in." I mean, the path was sort of carved out, and I believe Jackie realised she was in a presidential race pretty immediately. And, I believe, the point was that this became a fantastic endeavour that really brought them together... [and] they would spend many evenings... poring over books, hunting for lines that became famous after Jack used them.... And [their] study... rendered Jack a much more dimensional figure."

There was little time to consider whether they would marry seriously. Jackie's only statement regarding those mid-May days was characteristically enigmatic: "Both of us knew it was serious, I think, but we didn't talk about it then." The ambiguity of their standing was further underlined by what she informed Frank Waldrop before leaving the workplace. According to what he remembered of their brief talk, "[s]he expected to marry soon after she returned."

Jackie and Aileen landed at Pier 86 in New York at 46th Street on Friday, May 22, for the 11:30 a.m. departure of the SS United States. It was the world's fastest and longest ocean liner, having made its maiden voyage just the summer before. Jackie Bouvier was on her way back to Europe as tugboats pushed it from the pier into a foggy New York Harbor.

CHAPTER 19

PARTNER

Jackie was back in Washington with Jack less than 48 hours after enchanting the national press at Hyannis, quickly merging her life into his as he prepared to deliver his first public remarks as senator on a topic of tremendous importance to them both: France's war in Indochina. On Tuesday, June 30, Kennedy walked to the Senate floor and presented a long, thorough speech that drew directly from Jackie's substantial work for him. He was urging a revision to the Mutual Security Act, which governed the terms of $400 million in French foreign aid allocated for the battle against North Vietnamese Communists. The revision, he said, would "encourage the freedom and independence desired" by the people of the three Indo-Chinese nations. His case was "based on the irrefutable evidence of the accords and treaties," which Jackie had studied and compiled. Four paragraphs on page two, six paragraphs on page three, three paragraphs on page four, and two paragraphs on page five of his speech were all lifted verbatim from Jackie's Vietnam report. Furthermore, the ethical arguments and logical rigour presented by the former newspaper columnist seated in the diplomatic gallery staring down on him had inspired the democratic principles that rang throughout his entire speech. It was just him who knew, but it was enough. Immediately following the speech, Jack and Jackie boarded a plane to join the Ambassador in Chicago for a "Merchants of America Hall of Fame" celebration at his Merchandise Mart building, the site of the Ambassador's and Gramps Lee's spat. While Joe talked in lofty platitudes about the drive and advancement of the great businessmen who created the nation's leading firms, Jack's remarks were strikingly different, his Senate speech from several hours earlier vividly on his mind. "The greatest threat to a peaceful resolution of the issues in Southeast Asia is the white man himself," he claimed, possibly adding the British and Americans in his assessment along with the French. "This is because the white man has not recognized the desire of the people there, particularly in Vietnam, for freedom."

It was an unexpected take on the matter for him, but it proved his dedication to Vietnamese independence. According to the excerpts Jackie had translated, it was a sentiment she shared. Kennedy's proposal to alter the Mutual Security Act was denied in the Senate on July 2 by a vote of 64 to 17, but he was undeterred. He regrouped and waited for another chance to question the US government's backing for the Vietnam War. Jack and Jackie returned to Washington, and on Friday, July 3, Evelyn Lincoln noted that the Senate adjourned early, and Jack planned to go up to Hyannis to play golf. He ordered Jackie to meet him at the airport, but she spent the day shopping for housewares instead, showing up at his Senate office just as Jack was ringing to find out where she was, unhappy that she had caused him to miss the flight. Lincoln connected with Jackie on the phone. As he chewed her out, her face sank. After spending the Fourth of July weekend in Hyannis, they returned to Washington, where they joined the Bartletts and Senator Cooper for a buffet supper on Lorraine Shevlin's terrace on Wednesday. The gathering's headline couple, however, was Vice President and Mrs. Nixon, not Jack and Jackie. Pat Nixon noted in her diary that after supper, they all went to see the popular musical comedy Guys and Dolls at the National Theater. "Met Senator Kennedy's fiancée," Pat Nixon wrote, "a darling girl." Another feature of Jackie's new existence would be having such access to strong national and international leaders, which would provide an informal social arena for her to lobby on behalf of topics important to Jack—or to her. Friends also hosted a private engagement party for Jack and Jackie, which suggested to some that Jackie was struggling with aspects of her new life. "I think she was still trying to decide if marriage was the best thing for her," Aileen Bowdoin concluded after meeting her at the party. "I believe she was concerned about her life and future in politics." And she was still upset over having to give up her work."

On Friday, July 10, the pair returned to Newport. Jackie stayed at Hammersmith while Jack returned to Washington on Monday, and she was still there on Tuesday when she discovered that Jack had been hospitalised unexpectedly. It's unclear whether she had been informed of the whole scope of his numerous health issues, but it was upsetting to learn that her young, athletic fiancé of only two weeks had become ill enough to be brought to the hospital. The Associated Press reported that he was being treated for a "war-related malady," while the Boston Herald said that he had "recurring malaria chills and fever."

The Ambassador appeared unconcerned, and he was most likely the one who called Jackie and told her she didn't need to fly to Washington. That day, she travelled alone to Boston's Hotel Statler for a Bastille Day dinner dance, commemorating the "great French holiday" and posing for press photos with French consul François Charles-Roux. As the Ambassador most certainly saw it, it was an opportunity for her to make her first public appearance as Jack's envoy. Jackie was sent to stand in for Jack again the following weekend, this time posing for pictures as she went to Worcester on Sunday to present a $150,000 check from Joseph P. Kennedy Jr. Foundation to Assumption College, which had been partially destroyed by a recent tornado. Because she was uncomfortable being on show, the quick appearances were a blessing for her. She could easily get away from the crowds at the Bastille Day celebration. It would be different when she was with Jack. Their wedding had made that very evident.

The couple, along with the Ambassador and Jack's brothers, attended a housewarming party in New York for Jackie's sister and brother-in-law on the last weekend of July. That following, Jackie and Jack returned to Washington, then went to Newport, where they were feted at a dinner thrown by Claiborne and Nuala Pell, who were joined by Congressman Frank Roosevelt (son of FDR and Eleanor) and his wife Suzanne. On her birthday, July 28, Jack gave Jackie three jewelled bracelets provided to him by Tiffany, from which she would select one. While Jackie remained in Newport, Jack remained in Washington after Congress adjourned to attend Senator Robert Taft's funeral. On Wednesday, August 5, he set sail with Torb

MacDonald to, according to one newspaper, "spend his last month of bachelor life travelling through Europe."

Despite having publicly proclaimed his desire to go to France after Congress adjourned because of his "personal interest in the conversations being held on French Indo-China," Kennedy was chastised for going. "No man in love does something like that," Mummy grumbled to Jackie, encouraged by her columnist friend Betty Beale, who added, "I told her [Jackie] she shouldn't so readily allow that; she should have gone with him."

Jackie didn't respond because she wasn't upset—she saw marriage differently than her mother did. In fact, by embracing Jack's freedom to go without her, she communicated her own willingness to do so whenever she pleased. Their long separation, she would say in one of the few surviving letters she gave him, written some years later, forced them to realise how much they meant to each other: "[I]t is difficult for me to communicate—something you do so well.... I can't put into words how I feel for you, but I will show you when I'm with you—and I think you should know... "I think it's usually good when we go away from each other because we both realise so much," she wrote, admitting his reluctance to explore how he felt about her, while she was all too willing. "We are so dissimilar—but I was thinking of this trip that every other time I've been away, you would write 'don't ponder our relationship too much,' and so on."

Kennedy, who was unmistakably unromantic, justified his inability to easily communicate emotion by claiming it was due to his mother being unemotional and rarely expressing affection to him. "You are an atypical husband—increasingly so in one way or another every year since we've been married—so you mustn't be surprised to have an atypical wife—Each of us would have been so lonely with the normal kind." In times of difficulty, Jack and Jackie protected each other, but their first reaction was to protect themselves, and they expected the other to do the same. "She told a friend that she and Jack were both like icebergs, with the greater part of their lives invisible," Kennedy historian Ralph Martin later wrote. "She felt they both sensed this in each other, and that it was a bond between them."

Jackie was aware that he and Torb were chartering a yacht to sail along the south coast of France before visiting Sweden and England. It's improbable, though, that she was aware that he initially met and declared his love to a Swedish woman named Gunilla von Post while in the South of France. Nonetheless, he was not sexually involved with her, as evidenced by his letters to von Post. Jackie was certain that he loved her as he did no other woman. After Teddy became a U.S. senator, she later offered counsel in a letter to the former Joan Bennett, Jack's brother Teddy's first wife:

"Don't explain yourself sheepishly.... This is the twentieth century, not the nineteenth, when small women kept at home on pedestals.... Your life is as important as his; you love him, but you can't ruin yourself; you want a life of sharing... [not]... must wait in the next room silently while he and his aides discuss his problems—then he can have his girlfriends on the side.... You're not a prude or a fool... [However], men under pressure need to let off steam from time to time, which is why the Catholic Church holds carnivals.... What kind of woman, other than a sap or a slave, can stand that and still be a loving wife—and care about him and campaign for him like a dog? It's quite old-fashioned—he probably received it from his father.... "What excites me is forbidden fruit."It takes a far more real man to have a deep relationship with the lady with whom he lives. The routine of married life can become monotonous.... Leave the house.... Don't say where you'll be, don't refer to yourself as having a delicate health problem—don't ask permission.... Be a little mysterious—so he never knows when you're leaving or returning—when you may walk into the house at home returning early from a trip... Then he won't be able to organize anything around your absence.... Go somewhere fun with him.... Take him on overseas trips.... It will be difficult for him to tell you that you are unable to attend.... Don't let him think you're Old Faithful.... Take vacations with your pals rather than your family."

"Since Jack is such a fiercely independent person, and I, too, am so independent," she would say succinctly, "this marriage will take a lot of working out."

Marriage to a powerful politician would provide her with the grander life she desired. It would allow her to realise her childhood dreams of becoming "queen of the circus" and "Overall Art Director of the Twentieth Century." She, like the women of the eighteenth-century French courts who captivated her, had the power to shape history, whether she was credited for it or not. She might become both a participant and an observer of crucial turning events in civilization's history, shaping the narrative without leaving a trace. "You endure the bad things, but you enjoy the good," she would later explain in a letter to her sister-in-law Joan. And what great opportunities— meeting and getting to know important personalities, becoming a witness to history, visiting locations you would never have been able to see before. "You could never have such a life if you weren't married to someone like that."If the trade-off is too severe, you must just remove yourself or exit the situation. However, if you truly love someone, you identify it as an emotional issue that isn't about you. You will grow as a person by attempting to accept and understand these men as they are. Every day with them is misery, but every day with them is an opportunity to impact the world in big and tiny ways. You can have the largest impact over historical events if you aren't looking for credit, but this also provides you the ultimate golden opportunity of power without the responsibility that comes with it."

AS THE WEDDING DATE NEARED, Jack Kennedy sought advice on how to be a husband, writing to Red Fay with a wry but realistic tone that marriage could mean "the end of a promising political career that has been almost entirely based on the old sex appeal.... As I am both too young and too old for all of this, I will need several long talks on how to conduct yourself during the first six months, based on your actual real-life experience."

Jackie appeared to be more interested in soaking up whatever she could from the multitasking Ambassador as he stage-managed the wedding. The open-faced chicken pot pie, sliced ham, mixed green salad, hot bread, fruit cups, moulded ice cream, and petits fours would be served as a buffet luncheon. Countless guests were added to the list; Pat Kennedy's admirer, British actor Peter Lawford, contributed eighteen names of his guests. Jackie travelled to Fall River to place an order for the wedding cake—during his campaign, Jack had promised a local baker, Azarius Plourde, that if the occasion arose, he would ask him to make it.

Jackie hired a temporary assistant, Katherine Donovan, to assist her with the influx of phone calls, letters, telegrams, and gift boxes. Mummy attempted to assist with responses but warned the young woman, "My writing is getting worse by the day." Jackie should write them herself."

Aileen Bowdoin subsequently observed that the time between the engagement and the wedding "was a watershed moment in her transition from private to public life." I believe she was thrust into public life and quickly discovered that she was not enjoying it. She undoubtedly knew that too, but she made up her mind that she was going to make her mark and carry it off, which she certainly did. She was a strong-willed and courageous woman. She'd need it in politics."

Aileen, who would later become a political wife herself, realised the reason Jackie would put up with a lifestyle that went against her natural tendencies: "Never, ever forget one thing." She wished to assist in his election as President. I don't intend to be harsh, but she was very eager for the presidency, and he had what it took to go there, but she understood that he needed supervision, to be challenged on ideas, and to try to make each of his speeches stand out. She inflated his ego like no one else and was exceedingly protective of him against everyone. He had the goods, but she truly moulded them." Mini Rhea went on to say, "Just as Jackie desired a purposeful career, she desired a purposeful husband as well."

This unspoken acceptance of her intention to see Jack elected president was common among her acquaintances. "Well, if he'd just stayed senator, she'd have had a bad time with it," John White said. "But she knew exactly what she was doing." And, in time, Jack would admit that if he had been "unsuccessful in his courtship," he was unlikely to "have reached the White House."

Even in the days leading up to the wedding, the couple's intention was clear. Aileen, her sister Bow, and Martha Bartlett sang a song to the tune of "East Side, West Side" at a Newport party a few days before the wedding. "Donkeys and elephants strolling down the aisle," it said of the Democratic groom and the erstwhile Republican bride. To witness the biggest unification since Caesar barged down the Nile... They'll form a fusion party, rise to great heights, and win by a large margin—Jack for President!" The song was reported in the papers.

"Jack thinks continually in historic and literary terms," Gore Vidal observed, but he also possessed "the coarse energetic quality that wins battles." Jackie Bouvier was made up of the same components.

Jackie's columnist experience would prove to be better training for politics than it appeared at first, not just because her impromptu connection with strangers was exactly what she'd be doing on the campaign trail, but also as a "field course in psychology," as Mini Rhea put it. With her "adroit questioning of people," she "had really gotten to learn how people thought."

Senator John F. Kennedy strolled through the PanAm terminal at Boston's Logan Airport early on August 27, "fit and tanned," yet "obviously anxious to get off to Newport to see his fiancée," he paused to speak with Boston Globe reporter Charles Tarbi. He started by referring to his June 30 Senate speech on Vietnam:

"During Senate debates on financial aid to France, I introduced an amendment urging the French to grant the Indo-Chinese people as much independence as possible." On August 6, I travelled to France to learn how the French administration felt about it. The Indo-China relationship is crucial to Southeast Asia." He discovered that French opinion was highly divided, with some pushing for departure, some wishing to redouble the struggle against Communist forces, and a minority believing the problem should be referred to the United Nations for debate and settlement.

The amount of factual information in Kennedy's June 30 speech may have been too much for not only most of his colleagues, but also the journalists covering the Senate, none of whom mentioned the enormous detail he put into what was typically a staff-prepared speech. However, syndicated columnist Holmes Alexander had been noticing how much depth Kennedy brought to the difficult issues surrounding Vietnam, claiming that he "has done a commendable amount of fact-finding to reach his conclusions."

Based on an interview with Jack, Alexander wrote in his column about the "reference file" Kennedy was compiling on Vietnam, which included interviews with French military officials during his fall 1951 fact-finding mission to Saigon, books like Philippe de Villiers history of Vietnam, which he purchased during his trip, and even some novels, as well as current military and diplomatic analysis in the scholarly publications Public Affairs and World Politics. It was also in Alexander's column that Jackie's Vietnam report was acknowledged, however briefly and vaguely. "Kennedy doesn't read French very well," Alexander observed in a sentence buried deep within his fifth paragraph, "but his fiancée extracts the salient passages from the book and writes them out in translation." It was printed, then discarded. None of her engagement articles addressed it; instead, they concentrated on her wedding, riding, and debutante ball. Her vital contribution was not recognized until the 2014 release of her oral history interview (recorded in 1964), during which she disclosed her Vietnam effort.

Jackie began to appear more frequently in Jack's Senate office after the engagement, but the work she conducted for him remained behind the scenes. Aide Ted Sorenson remembers her visiting his Senate room and meeting with particular members of his staff, but he added, "Whatever political work she did for him, they kept strictly between them."

However, there was one individual in the Capitol Building who had a much better knowledge of what was going on between Jackie and her fiancé. When Fritz Carl "Duke" Zeller became a Senate page at the age of fourteen, he ran messages all around the Capitol—to and from the senators, to their colleagues and staff, to their fiancées and wives—and learned more about the lives of the individuals in the building than most. He remembered Jackie fondly: "She used to come to the Senate frequently and listen to the speeches, floor action, and votes." [She] preferred to sit in the diplomatic gallery rather than the wives' or family galleries. She would sit right in the middle, dressed casually, and almost no one knew who she was except insiders and Senate members. She was wearing Capri pants, a sleeveless white blouse, and a scarf over her head the first time I saw her.... But here she was, attending Senate debates!"

He remembered her frequently coming to coax Jack to join her for a quick lunch outside, carrying a picnic that they ate on the Capitol steps or on the grass. She would sneak into the Senate receiving room and ask Duke to notify Kennedy that she was there to speak with him. Soon, Jack would have Duke "take a note up to her in the diplomatic gallery... then it kind of became a usual thing." Of course, the page "didn't read the notes" but quickly "waited to see if she had a message for him." Senator Kennedy was also present, "listening to the proceedings [when] Senator Kennedy had nothing to do with the debate."

However, while Kennedy was speaking, the Senate page saw how he frequently glanced up at her, as if to send a subtle hint. "She was scribbling quickly, taking notes, then tearing strips of this long yellow office paper, folding it up, and having me rush it down to him while he was speaking." I'm not sure what she wrote to him, but I gave them to him right away, whether he was speaking or not. What was she saying to him? I'm not sure, but it had to be about the speech he was giving. It was only the two of them."

On April 4, 1954, nine months after his amendment was lost in the Senate, Jack's chance to revive the Vietnam subject arrived, and he did so with vigour and impact. He delivered a powerful address in which he demanded even more vehemently that the United States pursue policies that would hasten the country's independence. It would earn him the first national news coverage portraying him as a potential presidential candidate—and it would draw on Jackie's Vietnam report once more.

ON SEPTEMBER 12, 1953, Jackie Bouvier pledged her life to Jack Kennedy at the altar of St. Mary's Church, but their union had already been sealed in the United States Senate chamber.

Due to Janet's machinations, Black Jack was not invited to any pre-wedding festivities, but in the written lists of church seating, he was assigned a pew alongside his twin sisters and their husbands, two rows behind Janet and Unk. According to popular belief, he spent the whole wedding day confined to his Viking Hotel room, too drunk to participate in the ceremony (Janet had directed the hotel employees to supply a full bar in his suite). However, this was disputed in a news item published exclusively in the Washington Times-Herald, in which a comprehensive paragraph stated unequivocally that Black Jack handed his daughter away. (Because the press was not permitted in the church, the source could have been John White or another former colleague who was a wedding guest.) It said, under the subheadline "Given Away by Father," that "as the bride and her train of attendants approached down the centre aisle, she was escorted by her stepfather, Hugh Auchincloss." When they arrived at the third pew, her father, John V. Bouvier, III, stepped forward, and it was her father who gave the bride away." Usher Chuck Spalding, who was among the wedding party with siblings and close friends Tucky, Lem, the Bartletts, Red Fay, Torb, Aileen, and Bow, confirmed Black Jack's presence inside the chapel. Gramps Lee, contrary to popular belief, attended the festivities. In one photograph, he is seen cutting in on his old adversary Joe Kennedy to dance with Janet.

Joe Kennedy's meticulous media tactics had all come to fruition. The wedding elevated Jack and Jackie Kennedy to national celebrity status. Photographs of the bride appeared in newspapers across the country, including the top page of the Boston American.

CYNICS WOULD SAY THEIR MARRIAGE WAS ONLY FOR BUSINESS, that Jack needed her for publicity and Jackie needed him for his money and influence. However, their relationship grew stronger because they shared an intellectual bond and respect, and it was that betrothal that would anchor their own form of love.

Being "Mrs. Kennedy" was a public-private partnership. Jackie's purposeful, inimitable patterns of speech and movement; her personal charm and charming attentiveness; her scathing wit and burning irony; her flair and flawless taste—all of these factors contributed to the formation of her desired public persona. Her husband, on the other hand, saw her analytical, linguistic, and communication abilities as critical aspects in their shared, ambitious quest for the presidency.

Jackie desired to be in the Senate chamber as much as she desired to be in the chapel. She was motivated and inspired but never led by others in the four years leading up to her marriage. She created her own path. She followed her own advice to "figure it out as soon as you possibly can." Throughout this time, she was characterised by others in a variety of ways, from Deb of the Year to Inquiring Camera Girl, but she never compromised her most important identity: unique. In her own words, she had "become distinct." Jacqueline Bouvier was determined not to just observe history. She was going to make it.

The contents of this book may not be copied, reproduced or transmitted without the express written permission of the author or publisher. Under no circumstances will the publisher or author be responsible or liable for any damages, compensation or monetary loss arising from the information contained in this book, whether directly or indirectly. .

Disclaimer Notice:

Although the author and publisher have made every effort to ensure the accuracy and completeness of the content, they do not, however, make any representations or warranties as to the accuracy, completeness, or reliability of the content. , suitability or availability of the information, products, services or related graphics contained in the book for any purpose. Readers are solely responsible for their use of the information contained in this book

Every effort has been made to make this book possible. If any omission or error has occurred unintentionally, the author and publisher will be happy to acknowledge it in upcoming versions.

Made in United States
Troutdale, OR
12/16/2024

26625748R20093